KIDS
+ MODELING

= MONEY

How to Help Your Children Succeed in Modeling

Donna Lagorio Montgomery

Prentice-Hall, Inc., Englewood Cliffs, New Jersey 07632

Library of Congress Cataloging in Publication Data

Montgomery, Donna Lagorio.
  Kids + modeling = money.

  Includes index.
  1. Models, Fashion—Vocational Guidance.   2. Children—
Employment.   I. Title.   II. Title: Kids plus modeling
equal money.   II. Title: How to help your children
succeed in modeling.
HD6247.M77M66 1984   659.1'52   83-19199
ISBN 0-13-515172-4

ISBN 0-13-515172-4

Editorial/production supervision
and interior design by Jane Zalenski
Jacket design by Hal Siegel
Front cover photography by Tom Berthiaume
Manufacturing buyer: Pat Mahoney

This book is available at a special discount when ordered in
bulk quantities. Contact Prentice-Hall, Inc., General
Publishing Division, Special Sales, Englewood Cliffs, N.J. 07632.

Prentice-Hall International, Inc., *London*
Prentice-Hall of Australia Pty. Limited, *Sydney*
Prentice-Hall Canada Inc., *Toronto*
Prentice-Hall of India Private Limited, *New Delhi*
Prentice-Hall of Japan, Inc., *Tokyo*
Prentice-Hall of Southeast Asia Pte. Ltd., *Singapore*
Whitehall Books Limited, *Wellington, New Zealand*
Editora Prentice-Hall do Brasil Ltda., *Rio de Janeiro*

This book is gratefully dedicated to a number of people:

To our eight "model" children who have such a good attitude about their work.

To Lois Saliterman, who saw the potential in our children and started them on their careers.

To Donaldson's Department Store for giving my first child model her first job.

To Sherry McGreevy, art director, and Don Getsug, photographer, who gently guided mother and children along the long road to becoming professionals.

To Doris Fortino and Rick Carlson, art directors, and Tom Berthiaume, photographer, for using the children to their best advantage.

To all the wonderful professional people in modeling and advertising agencies, and to clients, photographers, and other mothers in the business for being themselves and making the jobs so much fun.

To my husband, Don, who suggested writing this book and assisted me with editing.

Contents

Foreword

I have known the Montgomerys for more than four years now. They are a diverse group: Pat, 14, Katie, 12, Tony, 9, and Molly, 8, have all been in the business for some time, two of the children for nearly ten years. Their father, Don, is inspiring because of his development as a professional actor, and their mother, Donna, is the organizer and business manager.

When we interview children at the Eleanor Moore Agency in Minneapolis, we look for that magical something that has to do with looks and personality combined. This is an objective not much different from that of other large agencies such as Ford in New York, for instance. The looks are wholesome, lively, and all-American. That can mean that the child has a tuft of red hair and the charm of freckles, as the Montgomerys do, or the sophistication of a look with blond hair, blue eyes, and porcelain skin. The client's demands vary. The trend for one moment may be for "real"-looking children, and the next, for the "pretty" child. No matter what the look requirement, the personality is the key to the final success of the child. Life has to radiate from within the youngster. The eyes must show the sparkle of the soul beneath the surface. These children are truly patient—listeners and followers of directions to the letter. They watch and listen and perform intently but with a naturalness that allows no inhibition before the camera.

Parents are the key for the success of this type of child. They must guide and nurture the child through success and rejection. The real objective must be to provide a balance between what is normal and real in a child's life and what modeling proposes reality to be.

A child must go to school during the day; that is part of the reality. The addition of modeling to the schedule can be exhausting for a youngster. The parents must exercise caution for the physical well-being of their child. On the other hand, the fact that the child may be competing with others for a job and may in some, if not in most, cases, be rejected, must be dealt with on a psychologically sound basis as well. Parents must be aware of the pitfalls of modeling and act as an anchor for the youngster, shoring the child up physically and mentally.

Parents should be aware of most children's willingness to please and try to understand their need to make their parents proud by "getting the booking." In modeling, choices are made by clients on the basis of the look or acting ability of the child. Some look for character appeal, others for attractive children. This is a very dangerous situation psychologically, because if the child is rejected, it may be interpreted as being due to reasons other than exterior presentation. The parents must guide the child toward a realistic approach to life, one not based totally on physical appearance.

Modeling can be a financially successful occupation for a youngster, particularly if the child is involved in television commercial production and collects residuals. The

Montgomerys have a way of spreading that accumulated "wealth" among the other children in the family who are not involved in the business. Their belief is that the working children demand more time and energy, so all eight children should share in the benefits they reap. The earning children in that way are the enablers for all the children.

Most children think it's fun and glamorous to be a model. But the pure and simple fact is that it is work and not just play. The child who will succeed does not do so because of being the cutest, but usually because of a professional attitude.

It is important to realize that being a successful child model doesn't necessarily mean that the child will be a successful adult model, too. There are height and weight requirements that must be met at a later age, and a child's career may be brief if the child does not reach these.

Most children in our market do better if they are small for their age. They then appear tiny and yet are more intelligent than their size indicates. But that may mean that they will not grow to be a 5'7" female model or a 6' male model.

We wish every youngster could be a model, and certainly every mother thinks she has a model child. Almost every baby has a warmth and charm that is loved by all. But the combination of charisma, bone structure, and attitude is found in only a few. That spark of life, eye contact with the camera, the fact that the child is a good listener and, most of all, follows direction are the key. And the reinforcement, nurturing, and positive attitude that parents can provide will not only make the child a successful model in youth, but, we hope, a productive and stable individual as an adult.

Andrea Hjelm
Eleanor Moore Modeling Agency

Preface

This guidebook of money-making success secrets will help you help your child succeed in a professional modeling career. You will learn what and who sells in modeling, what agencies and photographers look for in child models, and how best to manage your child's career. You'll receive experienced advice on such subjects as wardrobes, auditions, radio or TV commercials, and print work. Most importantly, you'll be informed about attitudes you and your child need if you wish to succeed in modeling.

How do you know if your child is photogenic? This question has been asked of several highly regarded professionals: (1) a respected commercial photographer, (2) the president of a prominent modeling agency, and (3) an experienced director of television commercials. Their responses will be helpful to you.

Building a modeling wardrobe is a basic professional requirement, but how do you know what and when to buy? These and other questions are answered in a chapter on building wardrobes.

Auditions or "tryouts" for modeling jobs are stepping stones to a professional modeling career. It takes years of winning and losing to know how to make the most of auditions. A chapter on this subject gives you the benefit of seasoned experience.

Your attitude and the attitude of your child rank first in importance with professionals who select talent. How you and your child regard modeling and how you keep a healthy perspective are major concerns. Rejection, for example, can create a self-image problem for your child. You will find out how to deal with rejection. Advance knowledge of the realities of modeling is helpful to you and your child.

Kids + Modeling = Money gives you advice in an organized, structured way. Headings within chapters help you quickly find answers to your questions. Stories of actual on-the-job experiences alert you to what's happening in modeling and what to expect. You will get an instant familiarity with the business that could otherwise take you many years to acquire.

From your first agency contact to banking your child's first paycheck, this book gives you useful advice from a mother with ten years' experience in the business. No other book has offered such advice. This is the first time it has become available.

Modeling is exciting and rewarding. Realize that it is your career as well as your child's. Then both of you be yourselves and have fun!

Acknowledgments

I acknowledge with deep gratitude the following people and businesses:

Andrea Hjelm, president, Eleanor Moore Modeling Agency, for writing the foreword and allowing me to interview her.

Tom Berthiaume, of Arndt & Berthiaume Photography, for the interview he gave me and also for the cover shot.

Randy Young, director, Northwest Teleproductions, for the interview and delightful stories he let me share with you.

Mike Paul, photographer, for the family portrait.

Diane Gale, president, New Faces Models & Talent, Inc.

American Federation of Television and Radio Artists (AFTRA); First Federal Savings and Loan Association of Minneapolis, Minnesota; Frankenberry, Laughlin, Bernstein & Constable, Inc.; Minneapolis Star and Tribune.

I would also like to give special acknowledgement to Barbara LaGorio and Lynda Warren for their tremendous effort in typing and retyping this book and to Joan Rose for reading it and offering suggestions.

Thank you all.

1

The Basics First

Almost every mother feels that her child has modeling potential, but a child model needs the right balance of a few essentials.

The child model must be photogenic. It's sometimes hard to judge your child's photogenic qualities from nonprofessional snapshots. But you can evaluate how your child looks in these shots. Are the pictures usually good, or do you quite often find yourself explaining why they're bad? Even if they're bad, you have to realize that as a professional model your child will be working with a commercial photographer. This person will see that your child has the best lighting conditions and that pictures will be shot at exactly the right second and in great numbers. Let the professionals judge your child's photogenic qualities from professional photographs.

It can't be said a child isn't photogenic because his or her ears stick out, or teeth aren't perfect, or hair isn't right. With a good photographer, a child's negative facial qualities often turn out to be attractive and salable.

On the other hand, a child may be extremely good-looking in person but may not be photogenic. Some quite average-looking children have become successful models because they are so consistently expressive on film. The reason is that they use their imagination to visualize the desired result. Photographers, modeling agencies, ad agencies, directors, and clients also visualize the final result they expect. So must you and your child.

Every time a model steps in front of a camera, something special should happen. That special something or charisma is what makes a child photogenic. It's something you can't put a name on or say with authority that the model is photogenic just because this thing is present. Rather, it's something that happens when we look at a person's finished photograph or advertisement. We see something that stirs us or makes us respond in a positive way.

That's not to say a child can't learn to model, given on-the-job training and experience. What is meant is that the successful child model should be capable of maintaining a consistently good quality on film.

The child model must be able to act. The qualities that make a good stage, screen, and TV actor or actress are the same qualities that make a good child model. Can your child listen well to directions and then follow them exactly? Following directions requires enough humility to listen to the direction being given and also requires the ability to produce the director's interpretation, whether for radio, TV, film, print media, or a style show.

Does your child like to pretend? If so, that's good! Is your child shy and uncomfortable around adults, or outgoing and comfortable? If outgoing, that's good! Children in modeling must do a lot of pretending. They must pretend that unknown adults are their mothers and fathers. This pretending must be believable, even though the pretended feeling might be different from the one they are actually feeling. For example, a child model might have to act and smile while hanging upside down by the knees, or work with live animals (wild and domestic), hold heavy props, and work in uncomfortable clothes in extremely hot or cold conditions while reflecting a mood not felt.

In addition to having the ability to pretend, child models must also be salespeople. Models in advertisements are selling a product. They can reach more people in one ad than a typical salesperson might cover over a lifetime of sales calls. Prospective customers need to be influenced and swayed by a model's performance. The performance should always be outstanding.

The child model must be well behaved. A parent must be careful not to destroy the spark of spontaneity that a child must have to be a good model. The photographer has to see the spontaneity and know that the child, while being well-behaved waiting for camera time, can respond when needed. However, there is nothing more disruptive on a job than a child strutting around, showing off, and being generally obnoxious. Children should be quiet and well behaved if they are to succeed in modeling.

This is also true of adults! During technical preparations for a recent commercial, adult models were noisily milling around, distracting the director and technicians. Finally, the director ordered silence in a firm voice and made it known that when models are not performing, "Talent should be seen and not heard."

In general, being photogenic, able to act, and well behaved are a few of the basics your child should understand from the beginning if he or she is to be successful in modeling.

The rest of this book builds upon such basics and includes the money-saving, income-building success secrets developed over many years in the modeling business. With the increasing interest of parents in child modeling and the growing competition, getting the right start and the right advice is essential.

2

Children's Attitude

Modeling is something your children can grow up with. It is, therefore, a way of life that becomes natural to them. For this reason, your children should develop a good attitude about their modeling. They should have no conceit or smugness. If they had these bad traits, you can be sure the traits would show up on camera, and the children would not be in demand for very long.

Agency Thank You

A recent unsolicited thank-you note from one of our agencies shows how highly a good attitude and professionalism are valued in the modeling business.

1-19-83

Donna,
I want to take a moment to personally thank you for all the running, lugging, ironing and "Super Mom-ing" you've

done for your children's modeling with *New Faces*.

All of us here appreciate your talented children—and we know they couldn't do what they do without a great deal of help and encouragement from you. Thanks for making our job easier!

Diane Gale

Modeling Builds Character

First of all, children will get a great deal of satisfaction from doing a job well. Photographers, art directors, and clients are free with their praise and support for children who work in a professional manner and have a good attitude. Good models are remembered and rewarded with more jobs and enthusiastic welcomes in the future. Children understand this quickly and know that not only is good work satisfying, it's downright rewarding.

Listening to direction, understanding it, and following through on it are excellent disciplines for all people. But child models who acquire these talents on the job will also apply these wonderful talents to their school work and home behavior. Modeling develops good habits for life if children have the right attitude.

Modeling is Fun

Most children really enjoy modeling, even though it's hard work. If they don't enjoy it, they shouldn't do it. Yet modeling is a lot of fun for a number of reasons.

First of all, if you have several children, your time alone with each child is really limited. The larger your family, the more demands are made on your time and the less time you have for each child. That's why you and your children should look forward to modeling. It will enable you to spend some individual time alone with one another. It's a wonderful bonus both you and your children can enjoy when you get a modeling job!

If you have a 10:00 A.M. shooting that will last an hour or two, you might like to take your child out to lunch. If the job is a little later, go to lunch before the job. The lunch is private time, alone with mom or dad. It's fun! That's why you and your children will enjoy the modeling job and look forward to other such jobs.

Physically, modeling jobs can be hard on children (adults too!), but most of the time, they aren't very demanding. Children have a good time and learn a great deal from the experience.

Modeling can also be fun when children do radio or TV commercials. If a part is a speaking one, your whole family can help the one modeling memorize the script. What a lot of attention that child gets! Then, if you go on location, you'll visit beautiful homes, farms, lakes, forests, and any number of interesting places. This will enable you to meet and visit with many different people from all walks of life. Educationally and socially, modeling can't be equaled.

Working With Adults

So many adult models are pleasant, easy-going people. They're also patient people. If your child is lucky enough to work with some of the adult models who work well with children, you'll find they can draw a great deal of talent from your child. By their example and expertise, they're often a controlling factor on how well a job is going to turn out! Adult models keep your children cheery. When a commercial shooting becomes boring, for example, adults can help loosen up youngsters by making them laugh.

On Being Seen

The child model's attitude about being seen in an ad is a bit different from what one would expect. You would think that children would be excited after doing a few jobs. They're usually not. They'll have fun doing their modeling jobs but probably won't care whether anyone sees their ads! They become accustomed to modeling and will probably react to it the way you do. If you approach modeling in a serious, professional, enthusiastic manner, so will they. But after a job is done, you'll rarely hear a word from them about their modeling.

Friends at school or in the neighborhood usually will not know that your children model, except for the fact that they often get excused from school. On these days their hair is all curled and they might look a little "dressier" than on other days. Children sometimes tease their classmates when they see them in ads. Such behavior is rare, though. If and when it happens, you can be sure that you'll hear about it. Usually child models are respected by their classmates, teacher, and neighbors.

Many of your children's ads won't be seen in your area. They might run in different states or in trade journals which the public doesn't see. Ads for catalogues, inserts, folders, coupons, and so on are often not seen in the area where they're shot. For these and similar reasons, your children may do a lot of work, but it may not be visible at all to your friends and neighbors. People are seldom aware of the volume of work done by a particular model, so there is a certain measure of privacy about modeling. Only a child model's immediate family knows the full range of his or her modeling activity.

3

Getting Started

When friends or strangers see your children's pictures in print, the first question they usually ask is, "How did your children get into modeling?" No one will ever ask you, "What else has your child done?" or, "Tell me about your experiences." Everyone wants to know how you get into modeling.

Find an Agency

There are two basic ways to get into the modeling business. The first way is to use the yellow pages of your local phone directory. Look under "Modeling," find an agency, and then register.

To register, call an agency and ask for the registration procedure. Usually agencies want you and your child to come down on a certain day and time, with or without pictures, to fill out some forms and discuss your child's possibilities. Some agencies register everyone; however, most will be honest with you in evaluating your child.

Your child will never become a professional model without representation by a professional modeling agency. Almost all jobs are filled, and almost all models are hired through modeling agencies. When deciding which agencies are good, the first consideration is money. If they ask for money, don't sign up! If a school is connected with them, and you have to attend their school before they will represent you, don't sign up! Check the agencies through your local Better Business Bureau. Call the local AFTRA (American Federation of Television and Radio Artists) office and ask someone there to recommend good agencies. If you know some models, call them and ask for their advice.

It's no secret that some agencies are better than others. If you register with many, it will become obvious which ones are best. It is better to register with a few good agencies than many inadequate ones.

It's also a good idea to drop by an agency from time to time and observe the action. Are telephones ringing on all the desks, or are phones quiet? Are agents working quietly or talking among themselves? You can learn a great deal from a surprise visit to an agency.

The second way is by chance. Someone from an agency may spot your child and ask, "Have you ever thought of getting your child into modeling?" When this happens, check out the agency. Find out about it from the Better Business Bureau or from another mother with children in the business. Agency invitations can be a very good way to get into modeling because agency people can spot talent and recognize a look that's right for them. When someone approaches you about getting your children into modeling, get the person's name, number, and agency. But remember: Never pay a fee to register your child.

How Many Agencies?

Child models are able to register with as many agencies as they want. Different agencies get calls for different jobs. Sometimes agencies compete for the same job, as in commercial work. But for print jobs such as brochures, coupons, newspapers, magazines, and trade journals, the client will deal with one agency. Often a client will go from one modeling agency to another to share the business. If your child is with each agency your chances of getting jobs are much better.

There is also the possibility that a client will want one specific child and will tell an agency to find that child. An agency can find a child through another agency, but few agencies are so dedicated in their search for a particular child. Make it easy for everyone to find your child and register with all the good modeling agencies!

The Modeling School Question

A modeling school isn't necessary for breaking into modeling. Unless you want your child to learn about charm, putting on make-up, or other such subjects, modeling schools are unnecessary for a modeling career. A modeling school in some cases might even hinder a young child because it could destroy the child's spontaneity and freshness, creating behavior that is too polished.

None of the photographers or ad agencies want a child model who appears too professional. It doesn't help to know exactly what to do or how to pose if the model does not possess a natural grace to begin with. Photographers prefer to tell children what to do, and can catch them in natural, spontaneous poses. Young models learn on-the-job from photographers, directors, and agencies.

Some modeling schools will put a person in touch with modeling agencies. Some agencies have a direct connection with modeling schools, and even operate them. But be careful. There are agencies that send students to their modeling schools and do a lot of expensive portfolio work. However, the aspiring model pays in advance for that work. In this case the pictures might not be useful at all or, if the pictures are useful, it might take years of modeling jobs to pay for them. In the meantime, such an agency usually has the adult model doing some kind of unrelated work. Girls who graduate from such an agency school could wind up selling household products door to door while waiting for a modeling job! Such an activity is not related to modeling and never will be related. The modeling school is merely a front for door-to-door selling, and a way to get attractive salespeople. Be careful!

Tired Child Problem

Every photographer who has worked with young children knows that they have to get on and off camera quickly. If a child gets ready and is made to wait 20 or 30 minutes, then the photographer is dealing with a tired child. A mother has to know if her child can handle this, and if not, wait a couple of years. Photographers are not willing to work with a difficult child.

Working Babies

Use your own judgment about the best age for your child to begin a modeling career. There is work for babies, but your baby may or may not like to have a picture taken. If a very young child has patience and endurance, a modeling career can be fun. Patience and endurance are essential when you consider that although print work can be done within an hour, commercials are booked for eight-hour sessions.

One nine-month old baby modeled in her first commercial, and it could have been the end for her! She was working with a man who played her father. He had to grab her in his arms, walk into the kitchen holding her in one arm, heat her bottle in a pan, and cook a hamburger in a one-hamburger press. After the bottle was done, he had to take it out of the pan, remove the hamburger, and walk out of the kitchen with the baby still in his arms. All this was to take place in 30 seconds.

In the first session, the baby worked three hours. She was very devoted to her mother and wouldn't let anyone else touch her. Every time the actor took her she would kick and scream. It was nerve shattering.

Here is how it was finally shot. The mother stood right next to the actor. When the director said "action", the mother thrust the baby, kicking and screaming, into the father's arms. He rushed onto the set, did what he had to do, rushed off, and put the baby back into mother's arms. When the baby calmed down, the next take was done and this continued until the director had a good variety of takes to choose from.

The production company continued to use the baby, so kicking and screaming didn't end her career. Infant children are so unpredictable. The baby had to be taken home at noon, given a nap, then returned for some other shots. It was difficult for the baby, the mother, and actor, and crew. Once the shooting started, the job couldn't be stopped. Too much time and money was involved. It was, however, an eight-hour nightmare.

Preparing for the Job

Before the job, follow your own checklist. Your child must be bathed, nails trimmed, and hair freshly washed and neatly in place with a nice haircut. A girl should always arrive on the job with hair loose. Even if a client wants braids, start with hair loose, curled or uncurled, because there are many ways to make braids. A client will have an opportunity to make a choice.

Find out exactly what wardrobe will be needed and then select it with care. Press anything that might be wrinkled. Pack bags with accessories that go with the clothes, such as shoes, socks, belts, hair articles, combs, brushes and hair spray.

A lot of time and preparation is involved for the mother. She has to check the wardrobe, iron it, transport it, pack the car, get the child there, do the hair the way the client wants, dress the child, put on make-up if needed, and have the child camera-ready and waiting quietly until camera time. Along with all this, the mother is also the agent, banker, and investment manager of the child's wages.

Hard Work

Modeling is not glamorous work. It can be difficult and boring. As mentioned with babies, print work is usually one hour, but can be more. Commercial work is booked for eight hours. A school child will "try out" for a commercial after school hours (an AFTRA regulation), but if a job is won, it has to be shot during school hours. That means your child will miss a day of school. Most principals will consider this a wonderful learning experience. But if they don't, and choose to refuse permission to be excused, a mother disobeying this denial can be charged with a criminal misdemeanor!

Whatever the difficulty of the work, a true extrovert loves it. And if you tie a modeling job in with lunch and other fun activities, it's special to you and your child. Time alone with mother and a special camaraderie make all the waiting easier.

4

The Modeling
Experience:
A Commercial

Audition Notice

Your child's first audition call or "tryout" will come after
registration with an agency. The modeling agency will
phone you. You will be told the date, time, and place of the
audition. It might be later that day or within a few days. You
will be told who the client is and what the job involves. For
example, if the job involves a farm theme, you might be told
to dress your child in jeans or bib overalls. Perhaps braids
will be specified if your daughter is to be auditioned. Photographers and artists can visualize your child in these clothes,
but a client wants to see exactly how your child will look. The
client will almost always be at the audition.

Preparation

Plan and prepare your child's wardrobe the day before the
audition. Try it on to make sure it still fits and give special
care to the child's personal appearance. If the audition is at

the end of a school day after recesses, art projects, and stuffy school rooms, plan sufficient time to prepare and freshen up your child's appearance.

Pick up your child from school at least one-half hour before you have to leave for the audition. Have your child wash, comb hair neatly, and dress in proper wardrobe clothes and shoes. Allow enough time for your trip to the audition so that you arrive at least fifteen minutes before the appointed audition call time.

Script Rehearsal

If a script is involved, your agency will tell you. Occasionally it's a matter of one or two words which won't be a problem. If a few lines are involved, an agency is sometimes given the lines in advance of the audition. If that's the case, ask the agent to read you the lines over the telephone. Write them down and rehearse them with your child. If a script is lengthy, and the agent has copies, pick one up if you can, or have it mailed if there's time. Rehearsal at home can mean the difference of your child's getting the job. If a script isn't given to your child until the audition, help your child review and rehearse it right there. Memorize it if possible. Always read the script over to yourself so that you can understand the thought. Then tell your child in your own words the story of the script. Next, read all parts of it out loud with meaning and expression. If your child can read, have him or her read the part out loud without interruption, then gently correct emphasis, if needed, to assure appropriate meaning or thought. You read the other parts. Re-read your child's lines and help your child memorize them if that's required.

You should be told if the script can be brought into the audition. If not, ask.

Audition

When it's your child's turn, he or she will be brought into another room and introduced to the director. The director will usually introduce the others in the room. Clients, art director, and possibly a cameraman will be there if the audition is to be taped.

To get the audition started, the children might be asked how old they are, what school they attend, or other such questions that put them at ease, inform those present, and enable them to decide whether a child can make the desired impression. A child's personality and speaking ability emerge and are evaluated.

A child might also be asked about previous modeling experience and what other commercials he or she has done. If the commercial involves eating something, the director might ask if the child likes the food. Also, the director will describe the job to your child. If a script is involved it will be rehearsed at this time.

The usual amount of time spen with this interview is approximately five minutes. This is why it's essential that you and your child prepare. Timing might run a little longer if your child is to be taped while reading a script, because there may be a few practice trys before the final taping. When the audition is over, your child is brought back to you, and another child is taken to be interviewed. You might be asked if your child is free on a certain day, or you might be given two or three possible days for an outdoor shot in case of rain or bad weather. You might even be asked if your child is currently appearing in a commercial that is being aired for a similar product or company. If so, it could eliminate your child from further consideration. Give honest answers.

Call Backs

Before you leave, you or your child might be told when the director expects to select the child model for the job. There may be a "call back." This means an elimination process, in which only a few finalists are called back to audition again. Don't be discouraged if your child fails to get the job after a call back. Be content with the knowledge that he or she was at least a finalist and his chances for the next time will improve with the experience.

Job Call

If your child gets the job, your modeling agency will call to tell you the good news. *You will be called only if your child gets the job.* Write down all the information and instructions given to you, such as the job date, time, and location. The wardrobe needed will be described. You will be told everything to bring, from shoes and socks to accessories. If you're told to bring blue and green clothes, also bring browns, yellows and even a red as well. Circumstances change. It's good to be prepared with a selection. Clients appreciate it, and it will help build your child's career.

A girl who is told to bring only slacks wouldn't need dress shoes. On the other hand, be sure you bring a nice selection of tennis and casual shoes!

Job Time

Be at the job by your child's call time. Hang up the wardrobe to keep it from wrinkling, then wait to be told what to do. If there's time before the commercial is shot, you will probably be invited to wait in another room. This usually happens, but it's possible a crew might be ready immediately. Use every opportunity to rehearse if a script is required. Otherwise, bring quiet things along for your child to do with you, with another child model, or alone.

Camera Time

As your child's camera time nears, the art director will approach you and your child and ask to see the wardrobe you have brought. If more than one model is in the shot, wardrobes will be color and style coordinated. Once the selection is complete, you will be told when to dress your child. After your child is dressed, and the set and cameras are ready, a mother's job is done. Disappear! Resist any temptation to watch unless discreet watching is possible and unavoidable. In this case, keep in the extreme background and out of the way.

The director will explain to your child exactly what is wanted. Your child must listen carefully to the director's instructions and follow them exactly. Many "takes" will be shot of each segment of a commercial, even if the first time seemed perfect. Tell your child to expect repetition. Commercials aren't necessarily redone because they were wrong. Rather, they're redone because directors and clients like to select from many film takes.

The job will probably last all day long, or at least most of the day. If the job lasts all day, lunch is usually served for crew, cast and parents. When the job is over, you will be asked to sign a release form and also a W-2 or W-4 withholding tax form. Have your child's social security number with you and know in advance the number of exemptions you wish to claim, if any. If you have a family partnership or other IRS-assigned, business ID number, do not use the child's individual social security number. Use your family partnership or business ID number and your child's name, if payment is to be made to the partnership or business.

Your modeling agency will receive your child's check within 12 days after the shooting of a commercial. The agency then forwards payment to you with the agency billing which is usually 10 percent of the initial shooting fee and 10 percent on all residuals (see Chapter 15). Be sure you promptly pay the agency billing if required to do so; otherwise, the agency fee is already deducted from the payment to you.

The commercial may be seen within a few weeks or a few months after it is made. It may or may not be seen in your area. In either case, you may want to get your own taped copy of the commercial and taped copies of all your child's commercials. Contact the firm that made the master taping and ask for their assistance in making the tape of your child's commercials. Be prepared to pay a reasonable price for the tape, then store it in a safe place.

5

What and Who Sells

Some children are remarkably beautiful, but don't photograph well. A professional model must *always* photograph well. Your child doesn't have to be gorgeous, but has to have a look that sells.

One day on the Phil Donahue show, Phil had an actual audition for a commercial. Five or six little girls tried out. They were called out on the stage one at a time, and a group of adults interviewed them. They were auditioning with a doll. The audience saw each child and could compare them. At the end of the tryouts there was absolutely no doubt who the winner was. One little girl walked out with stage presence and sparkling personality. It was immediately apparent to the audience that this child had that special radiant quality that gets immediate attention. She inspired a response from viewers that clients look for. This type of child will sell the client's product. Having the chance to observe a commercial audition is a rare and great learning experience for children and adults alike.

The Right Combination

If your child has a good look, is photogenic, a good actor or actress, well behaved, is able to take direction, has a good attitude, properly prepares, rehearses the script, keeps conscientious, and enthusiastic, then your child has a good chance of making it in modeling. Competition is great, and it's sometimes hard, or takes time to get that first job. But don't give up! Just when you're ready to throw in the towel, you could get that exciting first call!

Job Frequency

Most children work only a few times a year. This is more common than working every week. It's difficult to reach the point where the child is working every week.

Soliciting Business

Something adult models must do that children don't usually do is solicit business. Adult models have to make the rounds, meet photographers, and do a lot of "promoting" of themselves. Ask your local agency what is done in your own market. Usually children don't make the rounds. You wait for the first break, hope it has a snowball effect, and hope that your child is so good or so photogenic that photographers and art directors will enjoy working with him or her and will remember your child in the future.

Age Sells

Photographers have something to say about which models work. Given a choice of clothes, sizes 2T through 6X, a photographer will usually pick the largest size available for no other reason than that the older child will possibly be easier to work with. There is work for children of all ages, but fashion modeling is controlled by sample sizes. When asked what sizes samples come in for children, buyers at Dayton Hudson department store gave the following sizes. Infants, which include children from birth to twenty-four months, will have to fit nine-month or eighteen-month sizes. For clothes that come in small, medium and large, a medium sample will be sent. Samples for children in sizes 2T through 4T will most often come in those two sizes, as opposed to 3T. Popular sample sizes for older boys are 5 slim for pants, 6 for tops, 12 slim slacks, and 12 regular shirts. Young girls' samples come most often in size 5 for tops and bottoms, and size 10 tops with size 10 slim slacks. When small, medium or large sizes are used, samples will come in medium (10-12) for ages ten through twelve children.

Your child might model 2T for the short time that size fits, then wait until he or she can wear the next sample size of 5 or 6. That's why fashion shots usually start in earnest after age five. Product shots can vary, but given a choice, the older child will be easier to work with. Baby products are the exception.

These sizes apply to fashion modeling only. Other special shots having nothing to do with size are article illustrations, cereal and food ads, toy ads, insurance company ads, coupons, and many others. There's work for all ages and sizes in product advertisements.

Size Sells

The most active size for children is size 10. A great deal of fashion modeling for children is done in this size. Children's sizes go to 14. A junior girl may get by with a size 9, but she will most often model sizes 5 and 7. This may come easily for some girls, but there are others who have had their breasts bobbed and have started themselves to keep sizes 5 and 7.

As for child models, no one knows how they're going to develop or what they're going to look like in their adult years. Let your kids enjoy modeling right now. If they're a larger size, but put their health jeopardy to fit a smaller size, it isn't worth it. If modeling isn't fun, don't do it. When it is a great deal of fun for them, kids are good at it. Keep it fun!

Teens

Fifteen- and sixteen-year-olds who get modeling jobs tend to look twenty and are modeling as adults. Young teens who look like young teens are too old to model children's sizes and look too young to model adult sizes. It's a difficult age for boys and girls. They might be a little awkward, self conscious, or have poor complexions. Yet, stores that cater to the teen trade do use teen-age models.

Teen Makeup

When your girl is a teen-age model, she has to know how to use makeup. She should go to a beauty shop or cosmetic counter in a department store for help. A modeling agency might make recommendations if asked. There she can learn how to do the "understated" look. Teens sometimes have to wear make-up, but they should not *look* as though they're wearing it. Remember that photographers and clients are looking for a natural, fresh look.

Teeth

Children with missing teeth can have either good or bad chances for modeling jobs. Some clients will request them, others will request that there be no missing teeth, and still others will ignore the problem completely. As a general rule, it's best to tell an agency when your child has missing teeth or braces and when teeth finally have grown back or braces are gone. Agencies know what their clients want and are able to make a decision when you have properly informed them about any change in your child.

Attitude

Children must be in a happy mood when they walk into a job. Just before trying out for a commercial, you should remind your child to speak up and be peppy. After the reminder, talk about something else. Try to keep it upbeat. This is especially important for a tryout where children have only a few precious minutes to show a client what they can do.

Parent/Child Jobs Sell

Many adult models ha 'e children in modeling. These men and women must juggle their own bookings and wardrobes with their children's. It's an advantage when a company is looking for a mother-and-child combination.

Sometimes a mother who is not a model gets a job through her children while they are at a job. A photographer or client might ask the mother to put a hand or foot in a shot, or use a parent as a general extra in a commercial. You can expect a few pleasant surprises in modeling.

Another consideration in parent/child jobs is that your child has to be matched with the model parents in the ad. On a job, mothers and fathers are usually selected first, then children are selected to match the parents. This is true unless a child is of such special talent that he or she is selected first, and then parents are picked to match. This is very rare! Sometimes an adult model's children are chosen if they're the right size.

Height and Weight

There are two different rules when deciding which height is best. In commercial work, the shorter the better; in fashion work, the taller the better. Usually in fashion, a child will probably model a "slim," so a tall figure makes clothes hang nicer. For commercials, if a client can find a child that's four feet and fifteen years old, that's great! That child is going to be able to act, look young, and won't blow up on camera. Small is also good for TV work. Adult male and female models in commercials are very often small also. The client is looking for actors and actresses for commercials, as opposed to models, to show fashions to their best advantage.

For children in fashion modeling, slim is better. If you have a husky child, don't put him or her through the agonies of trying out for fashion modeling. Your child could get inferior feelings, lose self-confidence, and become very discouraged. There's nothing wrong with being husky, and kids do go through husky stages, but you've got to be slim to be a fashion model. Television adds a few pounds to you, so even then, unless you're doing character work (and that doesn't happen much with children), slim is better.

6

Agencies and Portfolios

Professional adult models need an excellent portfolio. This could cost anywhere from $200 to $2000 or more. Fortunately children don't need this. They just need some good head shots and an agency to tell them where to go to have them done. It can cost about $100, more or less, to get a good head shot. For very young children, you can start with a good inexpensive color portrait photographed in a department or discount store. But after a few jobs you will want a professional head shot by a commercial photographer specializing in head shots. One can be recommended by your agency. The head shot is usually your child's primary access to modeling jobs because directors and clients use head books to select children for auditions and jobs.

Head shots are not like child portraits. They should show a child's acting ability and camera response. Kids can ham it up and show a look or feeling that might be good for a certain product. For example, a boy will mug for the camera while wearing a baseball cap. Soft lights and a very delicate look on some head shots can show a different selling approach. Hands might be included if the child has good hands to sell. A photographer who knows how to sell a child's assets should be hired for head shots. You are not looking for just a pretty portrait picture.

Head Sheets and Head Books

All agencies put out head sheets or head books, but not every child can be in them. In fact, an agency will ask the model to be on its head sheet. Head sheets are important because they're probably the only way your child is going to be seen by clients and get work.

Head sheets or head books are done in different ways, then sent out by the hundreds to an agency's prospective clients, as well as to all the photographers. They're sent by the agencies at the agencies' expense.

Basically, head sheets are how models are selected. Occasionally a client will call up an agency and say, "I need a ten-year-old kid with blond hair and curls." In this situation the agency has the responsibility of picking the model. Since an agency's best models are on its head sheets, it's not going to take a chance on an unknown. When an agency gets to select the model, it will usually select from its own head sheets.

Size Changes

Keep agencies informed of children's sizes, because they're always changing. This is very important. Not only should you tell them the current sizes of pants, shirts, and inseams, but shoes, height, and weight also. Agencies have to know everything about a child, and their knowledge must be kept current.

Clothing Brands

Parents have to know in advance the brand of clothing to be worn on a job because sizes run differently. For example, if a modeling job is for an inexpensive discount store, the child may have to wear a larger size. It doesn't always happen that way. Some designer clothes also run very small. You have to keep up to date on all your child's sizes, including which brands fit and which don't.

When to Update Sizes

A good time to update children's sizes is when you shop for school clothes. Write down all the latest sizes. Usually there are a couple of sizes your child can wear—maybe a 10 regular or a 12 slim. In blouses, perhaps your child can wear a 10 or 12. Usually you can get your child into two different sizes. Be sure to phone your agency when your child's sizes change, and keep your own list of sizes handy by the telephone.

Be accurate. When you are called for a job, if your child can't fit a size, admit it. Also, tell the agency if you have any doubts.

Avoid Mis-fits

If an agency calls and asks whether your daughter, for example, can wear a size 10, and you think she's really slipping into a size 12, then you should ask if the agency can give you an inseam and a waist size. If it can't and you have doubts, say so—don't take a chance on a mis-fit. Answer your agency with a straightforward "No." It is better to give up a job than to have everyone angry with you for wasting time and money. The photographer will have to stop the shooting and reschedule. The client will have to recontact the modeling agency to find another child to fill the job.

Don't try to squeeze your child into something too small. Clients like clothing to be slim-fitting. They don't like any wrinkles; rather, a tailored look is needed. A slightly large outfit can be clothes-pinned on the back side, because it's what's up front that counts. No one sees the back of the model. But a too-tight outfit can't be easily adapted.

7

JobsAvailable to Children

The job market for children is so varied that it is limited only by an art director's imagination.

Newspapers

Newspapers are a popular medium for advertising. Children might illustrate a feature article or advertise a product. Fashion work for newspapers can appear in a feature article or department-store ad for clothing, furniture, or any other kind of product. Seasonally, a child will do newspaper work, such as back-to-school fashions, in the summer. Christmas ads are shot in the fall, and summer ads are shot in the winter or early spring. Colored coupon work is big business in Sunday papers throughout the year.

Department Stores

Department stores advertise in many ways. Children are usually included in catalogue work. Special flyers are made for certain times of the year, such as Christmas. There are also printwork ads and radio and TV commercials for special sales and promotions throughout the year.

Other Companies

Besides advertising in newspapers, many companies other than department stores mail coupons to customer prospects. Mail order businesses, service organizations, insurance companies, and other commercial and nonprofit organizations all use models. Trade journals are a good source of modeling business. Ads in trade magazines go only to subscribers in a particular trade. For example, *Toys, Hobbies & Crafts* magazine is distributed primarily to wholesale and retail toy buyers. Posters and in-store displays are also a good source of modeling jobs and sometimes pay higher rates for more exposure.

Covers and Billboards

Children do many box covers, such as those for foods, toys, and games. These are wonderful jobs because they pay more for the increased exposure. The same is also true for billboard ads.

Commercials

Commercials are full of children. Child models are used to sell products, fashions, and services, and the commercials are lucrative. The hourly commercial shooting fee for an eight-hour day would average out to less than the hourly rate for print work. But print work is paid on a one-time basis, while commercials come up for renewal every thirteen weeks and provide full pay for each renewal or "holding" fee for later renewal.

8

Job Variety

Sports Jobs

Child models occasionally have the good fortune of a sports assignment. On such jobs they might meet famous sports heroes. In fact they might even get to run and pass a ball, shoot a puck, or simply stand and talk with a favorite sports personality. Remember to bring your camera for some personal shots.

Also, your child might do a scene with kids playing baseball or shooting baskets. These shots are so natural for kids, they feel they're getting paid to play.

Tricky Jobs

The unusual should be expected in the modeling profession. Jobs often are tricky, challenging, and not what they appear to be. One job for a department store had two girls diving into a child's swimming pool. The pool was nailed above the shooting area at an angle, and tinfoil was put in it to look like water. Then long braids were put in one girl's hair so that when she jumped, her braids flew up, and it appeared she was diving into the pool. The picture turned out quite believable once it was turned upside down!

Illustrating Articles

Child models can be used to illustrate articles. These can be fashion, food, and news articles, or stories or poems. The variety is endless. Such jobs pay the standard hourly modeling rate.

Job Switches

Many times modeling jobs can change at shooting time with last minute talent switches and substitutions. A few years ago a boy and girl, who were brother and sister in real life, were to model in an ad for a window company. They had to sit in the waiting room of a doctor's office and read at a table while a mother model sat on a couch. The children's real mother had to take a younger daughter along because she was quite small and not in school yet.

The youngest child sat drawing on a little round table while the older kids were waiting for the shot to be set up. The art director liked the youngest child so much that she, with no wardrobe, became the foreground of the ad! The other two children and the mother model were background to her. It was a pleasant switch in plans, where all got paid!

Dangerous Jobs

Safety problems arise when seemingly harmless working assignments are downright dangerous. One commercial featured a magician pulling the product out of a top hat. A boy and his father watched. The boy was supposed to peer into the hat and then hop backward as fire leaped out. It was supposed to be a very safe trick because the chemical fire was not as hot as a real fire. However, something must have gone wrong somewhere, because on one of the takes the boy's hair caught fire! It just singed the edges, because of the nature of the fire and some quick action by actors and crew. Undaunted—well, maybe a little shaken—the boy resumed working, unburned hair back in place.

Animal Jobs

Animals and children in an ad can be a wonderful combination, but care must be taken to keep a close watch on animals in case they become nervous.

Animals on the modeling set can create problems. A large dog, if it is not well trained, might frighten a small child. Certain breeds of cats can be quite temperamental—even more so than some people! Or, a child can become tired waiting for such animals to perform.

A nervous cat, although usually tame, can become quite agitated when the bright, hot lights are turned on. Those cute ads that feature animals in children's arms can actually exhaust a small child who must hold the animal for long periods of time.

Then there are the "trained" wild animals! A local group trains wild animals such as tigers and lions for print and commercial work and promotions of all kinds. The trainers are dedicated people who love their animals so much that they tend to forget they are indeed wild animals. A job involving a tiger, Ronald McDonald of the McDonald's hamburger chain, and a little boy and girl illustrates the wild-animal problem quite well.

Ronald McDonald was standing next to the tiger, and the two children were posing in front of both. The tiger was supposed to hop up on a small slippery table and sit, but it kept sliding off, and this added to the tiger's nervousness. A great deal of time elapsed before the tiger finally got up and stayed up. Ronald was to touch the tiger's head and look down at a prop while the children looked at both. At one "touch" the tiger nipped Ronald's shoulder and drew blood even though the tiger was on a leash and supposedly under complete control.

Another time, a lion was arriving at a promotional event in a public building. A small 95-pound woman was jogging by when the 400-pound lion jumped on her in the parking lot. The trainers tried to control him, but when the lion decided to play by his own rules, even two trainers and a tight leash wouldn't work. The lion tore free and pounced, while the trainers kept assuring the jogger, who was by then flattened out under the lion, "He doesn't bite! Don't worry! He likes you! He thinks you're his girlfriend!" Comforting? As the trainers tried to pull the lion off the woman, it grabbed her tighter and scratched her head repeatedly. One cut on her head required three stitches!

An official who works with large cats at the zoo said that "bringing large animals such as lions to public places for commercial reasons is not a smart thing to do." (*Minneapolis Star and Tribune*, Saturday, April 9, 1983, by Dennis J. McGrath.) Remember, as the mother of a child model, all you have to say is "yes" or "no" to animal jobs.

Once a four-year-old girl modeled in a back-to-school commercial on location at several different houses. She was to pose as one of three girls on the way to school. From inside a house, each child had to open the front door, wave at the friends outside, run down the steps, and walk with them to school.

Each time the four-year-old opened the door and walked out, she got progressively worse. Finally, it dawned on the mother that something was wrong inside the house. She rushed up to her daughter, took her in her arms, then looked inside the door. There by the door was a huge dog, much taller than the four-year-old girl. The owner of both dog and house was sitting on a couch watching the whole affair with utter unconcern. The owner was asked to remove her dog. The four-year-old girl, however, refused to reenter the house again, and it took quite awhile to calm her. Luckily, the client could use one of the first takes. After lunch, the little girl felt calm enough to shoot the remaining scenes.

People get paid good money from production companies and photographers for the use of their homes for ads, and houses are left in excellent condition. Owners should be made aware before time of what to expect and what to do, so that they can be helpful. Any large pets, of course, should be removed from the shooting areas.

Difficult Jobs

A little girl model had to pose with a live chicken face to face. Before this she had to model alongside a live tiger, no cage! She needed a lot of courage as well as acting ability. Next came the job in a hot bunny suit, in which she had to carry a heavy plate full of eggs.

The little girl had gone through a series of difficult jobs including one where she had to hang by her knees. So, on her next job she suspiciously questioned her mother, "Do I have to hang by my knees?"

"No."

"Any tigers?"

"No."

"Any chickens?"
"No."
"Any hot bunny suits?"
"No."
"Okay. I'll model!"

Strenuous Jobs

Strenuous physical challenges which appear to be easy poses sometimes surprise a model. Sitting down while reading a book may appear to be a simple job. But if the model is sitting on her feet, cutting off her blood circulation to the extent of numbness, and is unable to move for an hour because her braids are tied straight up and wired to a pole, the whole picture changes! Simple instructions such as "lean in" can be excruciating in such situations. If someone in a group shot has to hang upside down, you can be sure it will be the littlest child or the child who tires most quickly.

Embarrassing Jobs

You have to be an alert parent to protect your child from seemingly innocent but actually downright embarrassing jobs.

An art director on one job needed a cover shot for a book. The cover shot was of three children in a bathtub. They were very young and all members of the same family. One wore a scuba mask and snorkel, and one used bathtub toys. To get bubbles going in the bubble bath, a vacuum-type hose was put into the water so that when it was turned on it made a loud noise and bubbles. After the machine was turned on once, the youngest child hopped out of the tub and never went back in. Instead she stood beside the tub and played. Her little behind is shown bare on the book cover all over the world!

On that same job, the art director decided he wanted to put everyone at ease and suggested that he, the photographer, and the mother of the three child models, take off their clothes so the children would feel comfortable! The photographer said that was above and beyond the call of duty. The mother gratefully agreed with the photographer and the art director was overruled. Most art directors are level-headed. This one was an exception to the rule.

Redo Jobs

Occasionally, you can expect to have to redo a job for one reason or another, and through no fault of your child. The film may have been ruined in developing, or the photographer might not like the lighting, or the client might want to try a different approach. Whatever the problem, the model shouldn't feel bad. If the job is re-shot, the model gets paid all over again!

When the Ronald McDonald House (for families of seriously ill children) was to be opened in our area, a young girl model was selected for the fund raising TV commercial introducing it to the public. She was filmed in color on a living room floor, drawing a picture of a house and a family holding balloons. Her drawings were reproduced as posters and displayed in McDonald's restaurants throughout the area. Some were transferred to large plastic sheets and hung over counters in the stores. The announcer told the public that the House would be a home near the University Hospital, where families visiting their seriously ill children could stay and preserve their family relationship with their children. Also, the announcer said that McDonald's restaurants would be selling balloons for fifty cents each to help support the House.

The young girl model had to lay on her stomach and draw while resting on her elbows. Even though her elbows were red for days, she never complained during the shoot. When the shooting session was over, she was happy with a job well done. Then came a call from the agency saying it was re-booking the job because the first film was ruined in developing! The young model had to do the job all over again. The good news is she got paid all over again, too!

In conclusion, you and your child model should be prepared for an almost infinite variety of modeling jobs. You should both be on your guard at all times, so that dangerous jobs or animal jobs, for example, don't catch you unaware and cause you harm. As a parent, always be on the job location with your child.

9

Building Wardrobes

Your child model has to have a good wardrobe. Using something your child already has is fine when first getting started. However, as your child does more modeling, you'll find that trying to use something you already have just won't work.

What to Wear

Clients will let you know what they want through your agency. On a commercial job models usually wear their own wardrobe items. For a fashion commercial, client wardrobe items are worn. However, even when wearing a client's wardrobe, models still wear many of their own wardrobe items. Your child might need shoes to match a client's wardrobe, or various accessories like belts, socks, and ribbons. Girls may need various color and style tops to go with a pair of pants, or various color and style pants to wear with a client's tops. There can be a combination of needs. Agencies will advise you, and needs will be clearly defined. Your agency will tell you what colors and what type of things the client is looking for. But be prepared for surprises. Sometimes changes occur at the time of a shooting, and items from your child's personal wardrobe become very important. Sometimes items are borrowed on the spur of the moment from other sources. Last minute changes due to lighting conditions, set designs, or other factors are not uncommon.

Wardrobe Fee

If a personal wardrobe is used on a commercial, the model will sometimes be paid a wardrobe fee. This is minimal, approximately $7.50. As a minimal fee it rarely covers what you have to go out and buy, but it's a little something extra.

Wardrobe Importance

To a professional model, wardrobe is everything. If a client wants something special for a commercial or print shot, go out and buy it because it's worth it. It more than pays for itself in helping you get the work and in establishing a career. Keep in mind also that if some specialty item you buy for a job doesn't get used, you can always return the item for a refund. If you use it and keep it, then you can write it off on your tax return as a legitimate expense.

Keeping It New

When a client tells you what wardrobe he'd like to choose from, he might say something like this, "We'd like some plaid blouses, some sweaters, jeans and some khaki type of pants, casual look, and bring a dress or two just in case, but very casual." When you're given all these descriptions, the client doesn't specify but means the clothes must look like new. If your child brings wardrobe jeans that are being worn to school every day, they're not going to work. Most children would have holes in every pair of modeling pants, plus grass stains on all the knees, if you let them wear their modeling wardrobes to school. A modeling wardrobe should be worn only for modeling.

What to Buy

Buy the look that flatters your child. When a seven-year-old girl, for example, is in braids, she can easily be dressed up to look like a little farm girl. So, buy her some bib overalls or plaid blouses to go with that look. When she's all in curls, buy her something not too frilly, but very feminine with soft colors like greens, blues, yellows, or browns.

Keep in mind what type of part your child will be getting. For example, if you have a girl doing mostly fashion work, buy her fashion clothes. A little boy that will be modeling playwear should have a wardrobe bought with that in mind.

Your child model must have play clothes and school clothes, but won't very often have to wear dressy ones. Also, some clothing items can be bought in a *slightly* larger size to get more modeling use out of them.

As discussed previously, you really cannot buy clothes that are much too big to be worn immediately, because clients want a very tight look. If you find a good buy in a larger size than your child is wearing, buy it to be put away for the future *only* if it's a classic style that will still be fashionable when your child grows into it. Don't buy too many clothes at a time, but try to be selective at sales and buy "classic" rather than "trendy" fashions. For any job, if a client wants something specific that you don't have, buy it.

Shoes

When shopping for shoes, buy vinyl when possible, as opposed to leather. New vinyl shoes look good, are sufficient for short modeling jobs, and are much cheaper than leather shoes. Buy shoes a little bit big so that your children can get more use out of them. They're generally just standing in the shoes anyway, so a *slightly* larger size is fine.

Special shoes that your daughter should have are the style of loafer currently in fashion, also tennis shoes, and white, brown, and black dress shoes. For either girls or boys, you could buy cowboy boots if the job will pay enough to be worth it. Get the inexpensive vinyl ones, since they may be worn for only one job.

Dress shoes for boys are not as necessary as they are for girls, but boys need casual shoes that are in style. The ever-popular tennis shoes are a must to go with dark blue new jeans. Remember, they should be kept just for modeling. They cannot look worn.

Colors to Buy

Browns, blues, greens, and yellows are some of the good modeling colors. A client will not often ask for reds, but a producer, for example, may say, "I want red," or, "I want stripes," or, "I want plain." What you have to do is acquire those colors at the start, then get a feel for wardrobe after your children are in modeling for a while. A wardrobe with variety is important.

When to Buy

At the end of summer, when summer clothes are on sale, buy wardrobe items to use in the winter for modeling spring ads. When winter clothes are on sale, pick out what's needed and use those items to model in spring and summer.

You can get some very good buys off season, which is one big break for you in modeling. The sales begin at exactly the right time for building modeling wardrobes. The reason for this is that you're always modeling for three to six months ahead.

When you see a good sale, buy wardrobe items for the future, even if they're not needed at the time. Of course, the clothes you buy have to be what is currently in style. Also, a model mother must anticipate trends.

The nice thing about classic wardrobes is that they can be handed down. Shorts and tops don't wear out like pants do. Modeling shoes can be handed down too. It's harder to hand down little girls' wardrobes. The penny loafer may be in one year, but the next year the baby doll shoe may become fashionable. There are different looks, so you do have to keep up.

Buying and Selling Wardrobes

Modeling clothes still look new even after your child has outgrown them, so you might consider selling or trading with other modeling mothers. Mothers in the business know that a good modeling wardrobe is worn only on jobs, so it's virtually new. If you can't sell or trade a modeling wardrobe after it's outgrown, you can give it to charity, get a receipt, and use the donation as a tax deduction.

Wardrobe Readiness

Keep your children's wardrobes neatly hung in their closets. At all times, keep items pressed and ready to go. When an agency calls for a job and tells you what type of clothing they're looking for, all you have to do is go to the closet and take out those clothes. Take out all of them! It's better to bring too many clothes than too few. You get to be known by how well prepared you come to the job. If you never have the right item, you're too unreliable for an agency to take a chance on.

You should have different-colored hair ribbons for your girls. These ribbons should be pressed and packed in a suitcase, ready to go. Have socks put away, also, because your child will have to wear good socks for a modeling job, not the ones worn each day to school that might have holes in them! When your child needs white sport socks they have to be new, not worn and gray. A model has to have clean, new-looking clothing.

Keep modeling suitcases packed and ready to go. Keep two large suitcases for jobs. One case can hold socks and hair accessories, another for shoes. You might like to buy under-the-bed storage boxes for modeling shoes. If you have boys and girls in modeling, one box could hold boys' shoes, and one girls'. Or, one could hold larger sizes and one smaller. Try to keep bedroom slippers, tennis shoes, casual shoes, dressy shoes, sandals, and boots in these boxes. Before leaving for a job, pull out the appropriate box. Everything is ready to go. If you're not ready, you could go crazy trying to get all these things together at the last minute.

Some children do a lot of modeling. If you have a child who is going to do only a few jobs a year, or who is just getting started, it isn't necessary to be so organized. Wardrobes, for example, need not be purchased all at one time. You acquire them as various needs arise. Many clients are very specific about what they want, so different clients can have different needs. Your wardrobe will expand accordingly.

If your children are making a TV commercial, and the client is very specific about wardrobe, go out and buy whatever you think is necessary. Don't take any tags off, but bring all the items to the job. The client has a wonderful variety to choose from, and you can return anything not selected that you don't want to keep. Everyone's happy then.

10

Auditions, Fittings, and Style Shows

Child modeling has changed since the 1970s. In past years, the same small group was seen at the same auditions, with very few exceptions. There are many more children in modeling today, and there is much more competition. For these reasons, it's important to have a good knowledge of modeling auditions as well as the business.

New faces are in all modeling job categories, but mostly in print work. In particular, new children start in sale catalogues or newspaper sale ads. These are fairly quick and easy. At commercial auditions, however, you still see the same experienced faces, and only a few new ones. When the "old timers" grow too tall to be in the smaller age groups, they move on to other types of commercials, so they're still around. "Old timers" who remain short still go to the same age-group tryouts along with the new kids, so there is a good mix of old and new models.

Although new faces are always appearing at auditions, the children getting the most commercials are usually the experienced ones. This is because of the time and money tied up in commercials. For these reasons, clients are more likely to go with the tried and true models, those who have already proved themselves. The photographer will also recommend a child with whom he or she has had a favorable work relationship. Also, the experienced child walks in with a little more confidence.

Auditions

Having a good audition is not easy. It's tough! Your child is going to have about three minutes in a room full of adults.

At a tryout for a TV commercial, for example, the client, the ad agency representative, people from the production company, a cameraman, and a director may be together in the same room. Your child model is thrust into this room full of adults, and has only a couple of minutes to show these people the talents they want to see. Your child must walk in alone, without a parent, and do all but perform. Many times the job will be already set up and your child will also perform.

If there's a script, your child may have time to go over it beforehand, practice it, or maybe even memorize it. When your child walks in, he or she will be "on." This is unlike print work where everyone can get to know each other. A TV commercial tryout is just a one-shot deal, and your child has to come on strong, speak right up, and not be bashful. It's very difficult for anybody to do this, but it's especially overwhelming for a child who's walking into a room full of adults.

As the directors in the production company get to know your child, they can do a lot to ease the strain by gently talking to him or her. Then, your child will walk into the room knowing at least one person. Modeling takes courage. It's a hard job and a shy child will have an especially difficult

56

time. Your child must walk into an audition with the confidence of having already won the part! The minute the director and producer see your child, an opinion is formed. They know if the child has what it takes. There is an open, easy, self-assurance a child must have when greeting these strangers. And when spoken to, the child must respond in a congenial, straightforward way. Your child needs charisma, the unique, magnetic, attractive quality that makes models memorable.

Handling Rejection

Kids seem to be able to handle rejection better than mothers. After the audition or tryout, put the job out of your mind. Some people keep calling agencies and pressing them for information. This ruins your image with agencies such that they may not call you again. If your child gets the job, you will receive notification from the agency. If your child doesn't get the job, you will receive no call at all.

When children are small, there is no rejection problem since they feel the audition is actually the job. A mother has to learn how to handle rejection. You'll never feel good about it, but try not to show it.

Print Work Tryouts

Print work tryouts shouldn't be necessary since an agency's updated head sheet is there for the client to see. If it's a very important job, however, the client might like to see your child to check for missing teeth, cuts, scratches, hair style or length and other temporary changes.

There may be a period of time when a child doesn't change too much and you might be able to use a picture for two years. There is the danger, though, that if the agency lets a mother use the same picture on a head sheet for more than one year, the child might not look the same in person. A client that has had a bad experience might then insist on seeing the children in tryouts. You really should have a new head sheet picture taken each year. When you walk into a job, you want the client to get what's expected.

It's a nuisance to go to a tryout for a one-hour print job, because you have the expense of gas, preparation of your child, school absence, and time. None of this is reimbursed. Unless it's for an unusually good client, you may decide not to accept. However, you should always go, even if your child has the job and is only trying on wardrobe.

Fittings

Occasionally models are asked to go to fittings because the client wants to make sure the clothes fit properly. The model gets paid a minimum amount, which is barely enough to cover mileage expense, parking, and so on. It usually costs quite a bit of money for a round trip, considering the fact that the model is getting paid nothing for the time.

Style Shows

Style shows, sometimes referred to as "runway" modeling, pay very little for a lot of time and effort involved. Once they start, the pace is frantic with no leisure time. Pay of approximately $30 is for a separate fitting day, and modeling on the day of the show. So you might like to do a style show as a favor to a client who has given your child work during the year. Otherwise, it costs more than it pays.

Your child might be hired for a style show that involves a morning or afternoon of walking among the people in a shopping center or other commercial place. The child might model for two or three hours and put in one to two hours fitting time before the show. All this effort is for the $25 or $30 fee—and that's *not* per hour. It's for the fitting and the entire show. For this reason, children who do print and commercials at a minimum of $50 an hour are not usually interested in runway modeling. Yet runway modeling can be a good experience for developing poise in children and good relations with clients.

11

Selecting the Model

Usually an ad agency that selects your child also represents the client. The client sometimes selects the model, but the ad agency most often chooses, and the agency's judgment is trusted. Many times it's a joint selection.

Prior to selecting models or talent, an art director from an ad agency will usually create a storyboard. A storyboard looks like a cartoon strip and does just what it says. It tells the story of a script. In print work, an ad is drawn on a layout sheet. The artist or ad creator will conceive the idea, write it, draw it and follow it through, possibly even selecting the models or talent. A representative from the ad agency will supervise the shot and see that everything is correct and blends together. It's interesting to see how often the artist's conception or drawing of how a child should look, is carried through to selection of the model.

In most cases models are selected directly from a modeling agency head sheet. In other cases, a client asks the modeling agency to select the proper model. Regardless of how the decision is finally reached, a professional model is usually hired through a modeling agency.

There are other ways a model is selected. A client might be talking with a photographer and the photographer will say, "I've got just the kid who works really great." The photographer's opinions, pro and con, are highly respected and can be a determining influence on a model's future. Recently, while waiting for his next job to begin, a photographer came out to the reception desk in the waiting area. He told the receptionist about a model he had just finished using and said she was excellent. After describing her good qualities, he asked the receptionist to write her name down and use her again.

Sometimes the client will fly someone in from either coast to be in a commercial or even in print. Many times local child models try out for these same jobs, but when all is said and done, the out-of-town model may be chosen for the job. This can happen not only with children but with adults as well.

In general, models can be selected in a variety of ways. The basis for selection is unpredictable, and the selection process is sometimes characterized by personal bias and outright favoritism on the part of the people doing the selecting. You can be confident, however, that your careful preparation, personal conscientiousness, and commitment to modeling will give you advantages over others.

12

Preparation and Timing

Catching Calls

When you are called for a job, write down on a slip of paper the name of the agency calling, as well as the name of the person who called. Note which child is wanted on the job, what the job is, when and where it is, how much time will be involved or predicted for the shooting, necessary wardrobe, and directions how to get there. If you don't know where a location is, don't hesitate to ask the agency for directions. Ask exactly how to get on location. Write the instructions down carefully, along with the name and telephone number of somebody to contact in case you get lost or delayed. Record the same information for tryouts also.

Using Maps

In the interest of punctuality and your own peace of mind, purchase a county atlas of your area. This booklet shows all streets and highways in detail and can be purchased at most news stores. It's so important to get where you're going in plenty of time. You can't afford to be late if you're serious about modeling. If you get lost and keep floundering around to get somewhere, it's because you failed to prepare. If you're not sure of a location even with a map, get an early start. Above all else you must be on time—that's fifteen minutes early!

Never keep clients waiting. However, they will probably always keep you waiting. That's fine because models get paid from "call time" on, even though they may be sitting in a waiting room.

Makeup and Hairstyling

Makeup and hairstyling are usually done by the model's mother. Usually, a child model doesn't need makeup at all.

In the wintertime, or sometimes in a color shot, children look pale under the light. If this happens, put a little bit of blush on their noses, foreheads, chins, and cheeks to make them look healthy. If the client is shooting in winter, the shooting is usually of spring shots, so kids have to look like they've been out in the sun. The season the client is shooting indoors is usually a bit different than the one that's currently outside. Makeup needs depend somewhat on the season for which the client is shooting. Of course, photographers can use filters to obtain the color they want as well, but makeup preparation can be important.

Very seldom will a client provide a makeup artist or hairstylist for children. Sometimes such professional help is hired for adults. When a client hires professional makeup help for kids it's usually for a special effect. For example one professional hair and heavy makeup job was done on a child because the child was in bed at night and the lights were set for a completely blue shot. The little girl was reading a mystery book in bed for a book company. If the girl hadn't had any makeup on, she would have been lost completely in the blue light.

Haircuts

A boy's haircut should look two weeks old after you've had it cut. In other words, an "in between" look is preferred. Too fresh a haircut can be just as distracting as hair grown too long. Try to achieve a happy medium.

Most girls have a better advantage with long hair. In the majority of cases you can leave it long, unless long hair is just not becoming on your child. Braids and curls are very popular, and long hair is more versatile.

Sometimes a client will request a special, unwanted haircut for a child—for example, a crew cut for a boy, when longer hair is the fashion. If you are put in this situation you should first discuss it with your child before accepting. Your child might be so embarrassed by an unusual haircut that the job could be a failure. Consideration should also be given as to how active your child is likely to be in modeling during the time the hair takes to grow back. In the case of a boy with a crew cut, the boy might not be doing much modeling anyway, and the crew cut job is a good opportunity. On the other hand, if the boy is working constantly, he might have to wait so long for his hair to grow out that he will miss many modeling jobs.

Permanents

Hair permanents are worth getting, especially if a girl has long hair. Without a permanent, curls get pulled out by the weight of the hair. In bad weather it's almost impossible to keep hair curled without a permanent, especially on a commercial shoot lasting eight hours.

Hair Color

With respect to hair color, it's important to remember that regardless of what color your child's hair is, a natural look is preferred. Just make sure the hair is clean and well brushed.

Set Behavior

Kids should never misbehave on the set. Their parents shouldn't let it happen. Children wouldn't have a chance to misbehave if a concerned parent were there on the job always. You'll find this out if you ever have to babysit a child model whose parents "ditched" the child at the job.

One mother left her boy for an all day commercial that took ten hours. It was summer, and everyone was on the front lawn of a church. The kids were supposed to be in a wedding party so they were dressed up and had to keep nice for a whole day of shooting. They weren't in very many scenes, but they had to be ready at all times.

The unattended boy in the commercial kept annoying the other children until finally he was told to go somewhere else. Other kids were kept away from him because he was wild and out of control. A large group of actors was there and all of them were disgusted with the boy.

This child and his parents violated the AFTRA (American Federation of Television and Radio Artists) union rule for radio and television commercials that reads, "Parent must be present at all times while a minor is working and shall have the right, subject to production requirements, to be within sight and sound of the minor."

For the protection of your own child, you really have to be on the job. You can't leave children to fend for themselves. The unattended boy couldn't be trained to break his bad behavior pattern in one day. The presence of one of his parents would have been a big help. Without a parent, the only thing the cast could do was get tough and order him to go somewhere else, away from the other children and actors he was bothering.

When you're sitting in a waiting room, you ought to have things to interest your children. Keep them busy with a variety of quiet things to do. For example, carry coloring books, crayons, scratch paper for drawing, activity books, and storybooks to keep them occupied and out of trouble.

Time Reporting

For print work, the minimum time involved is one hour. If print work is going to take a whole day, the client will probably give the model a day rate. That is a set fee, or flat rate for the day, which means that the client will get by spending less money. It can get very expensive for clients to pay by the hour for eight hours or more of print work. Your child is automatically booked for eight hours when doing commercials, so time reporting isn't as much of a problem, though it is still important to keep track of how much time your child works, in case of overtime.

Keep accurate records of time and see to it that all other models on the job agree with each other on the time worked. If there is no agency slip to sign, then go to each party in the shot and verify with each person as to when the shot was over. Then call in your time to the agency.

On Keeping What You Model

It would be nice to keep the beautiful clothes and other things a child models, but you can't. Sometimes it's permitted if the clothes are custom made for a particular model. Usually, however, you can't even buy the clothes your children model because they could be new designs out of New York, for example, that haven't been announced or even seen yet. Clients don't want such items out of their sight.

In one commercial involving three children, shooting time lasted 13 hours. The crew felt so bad at the end of this shooting that they gave each of the three children a large stuffed animal that had been used in the commercial. Then the art director came storming in to tell the crew, "You know they can't have those; they have to go back." He grabbed the animals away from each of the children. It was too much for one little four-year-old boy, who broke down in tears. Even though the children were tired, the mothers took the time that evening to stop at a nearby department store and let the kids pick out big stuffed animals of their choice.

Occasionally, children get to keep a toy from a modeling job but this doesn't happen very often. On the other hand, when children have spent a lot of time shooting a commercial, you might like to take them out and allow them to pick out a toy of their choice. They've earned it. While the money that's earned on a job is reward enough, it isn't always understood that way by children. A roll of Lifesavers or a toy means much more to them than the money.

13

Photographs and Print Work

Photographers are some of the nicest people you'll ever meet. Their usual attire of blue jeans and t-shirts matches their relaxed and friendly manner. Usually you will meet two kinds of photographers: in-house photographers and free lance photographers.

Free Lance vs. In-house

Free lance photographers have their own business and do work that is more artistic. In-house photographers usually work for a store that does its own work for catalogues and newspaper advertising. When in-house photographers work with models, it's usually a quick job. They don't take too many photographs. In fact, they might take approximately eight still shots when they use a model. Free lance photographers take as many as 100 quick action shots. Photographers can go through a whole roll of film in the time it takes the average person to shoot one picture. An assistant usually prepares the film and hands it to them while they keep shooting.

Professionalism

Both types of photographers are easy to work for. They'll help you through a job and tell you what to do. They can't stand any pretension and can spot it when they see it. Spontaniety is the key. A good photographer is the magic that sparks a child model. Just as a child must be a natural talent, a photographer must be a natural with children. If either of them is pretending, the job can be a flop. Professionalism, courtesy, and good conduct are especially important in modeling. Time and money demand them.

One job, involving a child model who was promoting a brand of fudge topping, lacked professionalism. A young boy model on the job kept sneaking spoonfuls of the product. Soon the client and photographer couldn't control him. The more the boy ate the worse he became, even in the presence of his mother. Finally, the frustrated photographer had to take action. He took the boy's picture and said, "And *that* one is for the agency." I'm sure when the picture arrived at the agency it had a note attached to it saying that the photographer did not care to work with that child again.

Professionalism is that service-centered attitude or mindset a person has that puts job importance and good people relationships foremost, with all energies directed to the best performance possible. The child model needs to be conditioned to a service-centered attitude and performance-based behavior by a gentle but firm "no nonsense" direction and example. The "cut-up" child simply won't get far in modeling.

Color vs. Black and White

Color ads in newspapers are good jobs! An ad is usually more attractive in color. Also, when it appears in a newspaper it's easy to get copies for scrapbooks. Copies of color work done for department stores or coupons look good in a portfolio. The paper is usually beautiful quality and the color is excellent. In coupon work especially, the quality of the shot is excellent, because the photographer has spent a great deal of time with the models and used many rolls of film to get an impressive selection of photographs.

Much of the work children do is black and white newsprint, and the quality of newspapers is bad. You might have to go to newsstands all over the city until you find good copies with clear, sharply inked impressions, but when you do find one good copy, the rest of the copies at that newsstand will probably all be equally good. There are also ad folders, brochures, color inserts, and many other types of ads that are fun to collect.

"Freebie" Jobs

A "freebie" is a job a child does for no fee. When a photographer asks to use your child in a studio portfolio, he doesn't pay you for that use, but rather offers you picture copies. That's still a "freebie" since photographers quite often forget to give you those "free" pictures of your child. If they do remember, it's so long after the picture is shot that the child doesn't look like the picture anymore, so it cannot be used for a portfolio. When adult models use children in portfolios, they pay the hourly rate. If a model will pay, a photographer should also.

Job Comfort

Children can plan on modeling snowsuits in July and sunsuits in December! In winter you try to keep kids warm as they model swim suits and light summer clothing. In July, when it's 95°, models will go to a studio that's not air-conditioned and model snowmobile suits under blistering hot lights. They really earn their money several times over on these jobs.

Underwear Ads

Fashion work includes modeling for underwear ads. Children are asked if they would be comfortable modeling underclothes. All ads of this type, faces showing or not, pay double the hourly rate. Thus, if your child earns $50 an hour, a one-hour underwear ad will pay $100.
dollars.

Overexposure

Too much exposure of a single ad is not always good, because a child is only paid once and may become too familiar to the public to use on other ads. For example, billboard ads, if used for a long time can wear out the unique look of your child model. There's a special billboard rate because of the overexposure problem, but if the ad runs too long, the extra pay never compensates you for the potential earnings loss. For this reason, many models will write a "good for one year" use limitation on a release form before signing it. This is a good idea and may come into widespread use if print work modeling becomes unionized, and residuals are paid for prolonged ad usages.

Happy/Sad Shots

Have you ever wondered how those happy/sad shots are done? In one ad, little preschool children were supposed to look sad wearing barrels, and then look happy in a beautiful snowsuit. First the snowsuit was worn for the happy shot. Then the snowsuit was taken off and a barrel with red suspenders was put on each child over underpants only. No one had to tell the toddlers to look sad. All of a sudden a very sad pucker appeared on the faces of all the children and tears were not far behind.

Sets

Sets for print or commercial work can be very elaborate. Set carpenters create rooms, attics, homes, and even outdoor scenes. In one print job for a window company, the ad had a big sister playing a clarinet in the background of a living room. Her little stage brother was looking out of the window, watching for dad to come home. The entire front of a house with bay window was in the studio, and a living room was created behind it. It was so authentic that a tree branch and light were propped out of picture range so that leaves could be reflected on the window of the house and the girl in the background could be in a natural looking shadow. It really looked like 5:00 P.M. sunset when their father would be coming home. The set demonstrated an exceptional observance of detail.

Planning the Job

For print work you'll get a call from your agency. They'll tell you where and when to go and the modeling wardrobe you are to bring. Sometimes the client will supply the wardrobe, but most of the time you bring your own. Be sure you bring enough!

On a job involving adults and children, one man came in with almost every piece of clothing he owned. The crew was laughing and teasing him, and he was the butt of many jokes. But he had the last laugh. When the other adults in the scene showed their wardrobes, each had brought only a few items. Nothing was right. The art director kept going to the one fellow they had made fun of, borrowing parts of his wardrobe. As it ended up, he used quite a bit of his wardrobe to help out the others. It's better to be laughed at for having too much than too little!

The well prepared often have socks, hair accessories, shirts, or shoes borrowed from them. This is because through experience they learn what to bring, while others often lack this knowledge. Wardrobe is very important.

Timing

You can plan that a print job will last one hour unless you are told differently by your agent. This is because the client is paying the child hourly for print work and not the daily time rate that TV commercials are paying. If the client is paying your child $50 per hour, the production crew is going to work quickly.

Arrive Early

Plan to arrive at a job 15 minutes ahead of call time with wardrobe. That gives the art director time to select items from your child's wardrobe. Quickly help your child dress, and stand ready for the shot. "Stand ready" means just that.

The client doesn't want any wrinkles in the clothes! Also, prepare your child model to wait patiently for the photographer, who may be busy making last minute lighting and filming arrangements.

The Job Begins

Before stepping onto the set, the model wipes his or her shoes, and steps carefully onto the set location indicated by the photographer or director. The photographer or director then tells the model what is required in the shootings. The art director sometimes shows the model the layout so the model knows how to stand and pose. Good print ads require as much acting and reacting as commercials.

Polaroids

Polaroids are shot first to check lighting adjustments, picture content, and areas to be filled, and so on. This kind of preparation is time consuming, but once everything comes together the shooting is over quickly.

Releases

When your child is through modeling, you must be sure you sign the release. The release is a form required of every model authorizing use of the model's photograph for the ad. Also, you may want to write in a time limit, for example, "Good through 19—" (put in the current year) to prevent overexposure of a shooting for which they were paid only once.

MODEL RELEASE

Time Arrived: _____   Hourly Rate: _____

Departed: _____   Total: _____

In consideration for value received, receipt whereof is acknow-
ledged, I hereby give _____ the
absolute right and permission to copyright and/or publish, or
use photographic portraits or pictures of me, or in which I may
be included in whole or in part, or composite or distorted in
character or form, in conjunction with my own or a fictitious
name, or reproductions thereof in color or otherwise, made through
any media at this studio or elsewhere, for art, advertising, trade,
or any other lawful purpose whatsoever.

I hereby waive any right that I may have to inspect and/or approve
the finished product or the advertising copy that may be used in
connection therewith, or the use to which it may be applied.

I hereby release, discharge, and agree to save _____
from any liability by virtue of any blurring, distortion, alteration,
optical illusion, or in composite form, whether intentional or
otherwise, that may occur or be produced in the taking of said
pictures, or in any processing tending toward the completion of
the finished product.

                          Date: _____

Model: _____
Address: _____

       _____

Parent or Guardian: _____
Witness: _____

Releases must be signed for everything that a model does, print or commercial. The model, or the parent or guardian if the model is a minor, also signs W-2 forms for taxes when doing a commercial. Releases may have a new format shortly, since more models are writing in their own terms. For example, a model might sign a release and write on it that the shot "may be used for one year only," or write down specifically what it may be used for. This makes good sense and is a way of discouraging any unauthorized use.

Requesting Copies

After completing the release, your child will quickly change back to street clothes and you'll be ready to leave. Before leaving, find out what the photographs, tapes, or film will be used for, when, where, and if you may receive a copy or copies. If an ad isn't easily accessible in the newspapers or magazines, as in the case of a brochure or store display, for example, the client is usually more than happy to take your name and address and send you copies. Since much modeling work is for out of town use in trade journals or mailers, you wouldn't find ad copies any other way than through the client. If a client forgets to send you one or more copies of an ad, don't hesitate to phone your request. Some have asked for ad copies six months after a job and the client was happy to send them.

Payment

Models get paid by the hour for print work. There are exceptions such as billboards, box covers, brochures or other usages where the model gets heavy exposure. For example, billboard and box cover ads pay five times the hourly rate, plus the total number of hours the job took to shoot. If the rate is $50 per hour and the child worked two hours, payment would be five times the hourly rate, or $250, plus $50 for each of the two hours worked, which is another $100, or a total of $350.

Sometimes a modeling agency splits the rates paid to child models into groups. A child up to age six might get one rate, then until age 12 a higher rate is set. From age 12 to 16 or adulthood, a child is paid at still another rate. Out of that pay rate, the agency takes its commission, which can be anywhere from a minimum of 15 percent to 32 percent. The agencies have many creative ways of arriving at their fee. The bottom line is that kids usually end up with the same net amount from all agencies, no matter what the cut is that the agency takes from the client. What an agency charges a client is the individual agency's concern. The important point here is that payment from the agency to the model is almost always consistent. Timing of the payment is another matter.

It usually takes a few months to receive a paycheck for print work. The pecking order of payments takes time. First, an ad agency bills the client and waits for the client to pay. Then the ad agency pays the model agency. Finally, the model agency pays the talent. By the time you complete that circle, give or take a few organizations and depending on how quickly people pay, two to three months have elapsed. When five months have elapsed, call the agency to ask them if they'll check on a delinquent account. Five months is much too long for a model to have to wait for payment. When times are hard, and everybody is worrying about cash flow, the talent, unfortunately, is always the one that seems to suffer the most.

14

Radio and TV Production

Voice-Over Work

Models do a lot of "voice-over" work. It can be for either TV or radio. The radio actor works entirely with a script. The script is given out ahead of time by as much as a day or more, or as little as ten minutes before rehearsal. Be prepared for any timing.

If a child is too young to read, or doesn't read very well, have the child memorize the script. Most children have very quick minds for memorizing. If your child reads a little, it might be wise to have the script handy to glance over after it is memorized.

Shown on the following pages are two examples of scripts. One is a radio script with a Christmas message. The other is a television script involving a father and daughter discussing what to get the mother for Christmas.

Giggling on Cue

There is an amusing story involving radio voice-over work that illustrates a whole family's dedication to the business. The script was not involved, rather, children's voices were to be recorded in natural, spontaneous laughter. The audition required that the children simply giggle on cue. The client had a "tickle" room in one of its large local department stores. A child was needed to giggle in the background while a woman read a script.

Each child was brought into a huge room at the advertising agency. It was black, with black furniture, including a black chair and black desk and wasn't the type of room you would think could encourage laughter.

Usually a mother never goes into a tryout with a child. Your child has to face all those sharp-eyed people alone. This particular time the mothers were invited in because the client was basically searching for ideas, and the children were quite young. The client, a woman, asked each child to laugh. One girl gave her a little giggle, but it was nothing spectacular. Her mother also had a boy at home who was a real giggler. She suggested that perhaps she could bring both daughter and son. If the girl couldn't giggle, maybe the boy would. In the meantime, the mother told the client she would think of something to make them laugh. Both kids got the job!

The night before going downtown for the recording session, the mother talked to one of her older teenage daughters. She asked her what could be done to make the children laugh. The teenager and mother both started looking through some magazines for funny pictures and found an ad for panty hose with all sizes of ladies: fat, skinny, short and tall. The picture was quite funny and was cut out for a prop. Then they found another picture of a bald-headed girl and also cut that one out. The family went to the studio with two amusing pictures that hadn't been seen by the children, who were to giggle on cue. At the right time in the recording booth, the teenager was to flash them at the children to get some laughs.

While the children's father parked the car, the mother, teenage daughter, and child models walked up to the studio office. Approaching the studio, the mother said to the teenager, "What we really need is a *Playboy* magazine." She had heard that there were lots of nudes in that magazine and little kids always seem to break out laughing when they see nudes. It was decided that if a *Playboy* magazine was available they would use it as a last resort, a sort of grand finale.

Inside the studio office, there was a table and only one magazine on it. It was *Playboy*! The mother grabbed the magazine and started looking through it. After getting over the initial shock at what she saw, she found a rather conservative-looking backside view of a woman nude. Nothing risque, mind you, but something that would make the children giggle. She told her teenage daughter, "This is the third picture, this is our grand finale."

They went into the studio and the crew was all set up. The child models were talking and laughing. The producer said, "Let's get them into the control room, they're in a great mood!" He got the kids in the booth and their mother asked if her teenage daughter could go in with the children. He said, "Sure." They had the three surprise pictures all lined up: first, the panty hose, second, the bald-headed woman, finally, the *Playboy* shot of the female nude backside.

The children sat in the booth together. Their teenage sister showed them the panty hose shot. They started laughing. It was so spontaneous, all started to laugh.

Then, when the first peals of laughter started dying down, their teenage sister held up the bald-headed woman picture. Another round of laughing burst forth with enthusiastic giggles.

Finally, when the second round of laughter began to fade, their teenage sister held up the *Playboy* magazine photo of the female nude backside and both children nearly collapsed on the floor with wild laughing. It was a grand finale.

All three rounds of laughing took about 30 seconds! The producer said, "Cut, we've got all the tape we'll ever need, it's fantastic! Just when we thought they couldn't laugh anymore, we got even more laughter, better than the last."

It was an excellent recording session and everyone was out of the control booth within a minute. When the children's father walked in after having just parked the car, the job was done. He couldn't believe the session went so quickly.

Later, instead of cutting one child out, the client liked the recording so much that both children were used in the ad. It was possible for one child's laughter to have been cut. Miracles can be achieved by sound technicians in a recording studio: a flat singer can be made to sing one key, one instrument can be made to sound like a band; or one singer, a chorus. So too could one of the children's voices have been cut from the recording of two. The client originally wanted only one, but decided not to separate the two. Both child models got paid and the whole family helped with the job.

Most voice-over work is done within an hour, and it pays well, too. If your kids have nice, clear voices, voice-over work can be well worth your effort. Remember, however, that preparation is very important, and often it's necessary to be innovative, creative, and adaptive to get the right reactions.

The following is a sample radio script sponsored by a bank. It involved one six-year-old girl reading an excerpt from Dickens' *A Christmas Carol*. The only other voice is the announcer at the close identifying the client.

Girl: Scrooge dressed himself all in his best, and at last got out into the street. The people were by this time pouring forth, as he had seen them with the Ghost of Christmas Present. And walking with his hands behind him, Scrooge regarded every one with a delighted smile. He looked so irresistably pleasant that three of four good-humored fellows said: "Good morning, sir. A merry Christmas to you." And Scrooge said often afterwards, that of all the happy sounds he had ever heard, these were the happiest in his ears.

And ever afterwards it was always said of him that he knew how to keep Christmas well. And so, as Tiny Tim observed, God bless us, every one.

Announcer: This special Christmas message was brought to you by First Federal Savings.

The following is a television script. Audio and video are separated.

VIDEO	AUDIO	
Up on little girl in family room. Father enter frame.	Dad:	Evelyn, want to go to Prange's with me and get Mom a Christmas present?
	Girl:	Let's get her something extra special.
	Dad:	Any ideas?
	Girl:	How about a baby sister?
	Anncr:	(PRODUCT)
They come in front door, carrying presents.	Girl:	Do you think Mommy will like what we got her at Prange's?
	Dad:	Mmm-hmmm.
	Girl:	'Cause they're extra special?
Father tweaks her nose. They hug.	Dad:	And 'cause they're from someone extra special.

Production Crews

Production crews consist of technicians who help make commercials. When you walk into a production company, you'll meet people who will be working the camera, plus a director on the set who will be connected with a control room if the commercial is to be video taped. Whatever the function, you can expect to work with a crew of highly trained technicians who know exactly what is required of them and how best to do it. When you're on a job with these technicians, it's important to sit quietly in the background with your child and wait patiently for camera time. There's much preparation by the production crew before anyone gets in front of a camera. The model's time in front of the camera is usually less than the set-up time.

If your child is lucky enough to get a commercial, the production crew for that commercial will be paying your child for a full eight hours. The shooting day might be from 8:00 in the morning until 5:00 P.M., with an hour off for lunch. During that time you and your child will sit for hours and hours. He or she might be on camera for an hour or less, or for most of the day, depending on how many scenes are shot and how many your child is in. You will definitely be sitting and waiting for awhile, because the crew is getting everything set up. They have a storyboard to follow, so they know just what shots they're going to do and how to do them. Sometimes, they're even constructing props or painting backdrops.

Production crews usually wear jeans and casual shirts. They're an informal group except when it comes to their work. At that they're professional, exacting, and know specifically what they need to do and how to do it.

Food Stylists

Among the more interesting jobs is that of the food stylist. Food stylists are clever people who make all the food we see in ads so appetizing. But you wouldn't really want to eat the food used in an ad. It might have hair spray on it, or a fake middle in a pie, or oil for a glossy look. These are just a few special effects. Some items, of course, are perfectly edible, but most food styling is really quite creative and dangerous to your health!

Eating Food

When children and adults have to eat food in a commercial, it isn't possible or reasonable for them to keep eating food throughout a series of takes. Commercials are shot in a series of seconds—possibly three and a half seconds for the first scene, two seconds for the second scene, and so on. For example your child may have to take a big mouthful of food for a three and a half second shot. When the director says "cut," your child will be given a bag so that the food can be disposed of without having to swallow it.

Structured Time

During TV commercial set up times you must exercise patience. This is what makes or breaks a model. A mother who leaves her child at the studio door and says, "I have my own career to take care of," then goes off, leaving her child alone to flounder for eight hours, is courting disaster. No one, not even a mother, can sit quietly and occupy herself for long periods of time without the time being structured.

"Structured" time means that children and parents find quiet things to do, such as playing little battery-operated computer games, coloring books, playing cards, or anything else that's fun and can be done together. You and your child are probably going to be sitting for quite awhile in a waiting room. You both have to be quiet. If you are also having to deal with a child left at the door while the mother or father scoots out, you will be babysitting an extra child. The time has to be well planned. The production crews are doing their work, and you're to occupy yourselves quietly, keeping out of the way until camera time.

Height Considerations

Much of the time, adults in TV commercials are shorter than those in fashion print work. If a client wants a wash machine, refrigerator or TV to look large, a small model may be picked to accomplish that objective. A child who is tall may no longer do toy commercials. If a client has a sandbox-size truck, for example, he'll pick a small child to enhance its size. If the commercial involves tiny pocket cars, then the bigger the children in the commercial, the smaller the cars look. Therefore, a tall child would have a much better chance than a small child to get such a commercial.

Locations

Commercials are almost always shot locally. If they are out of state, your child will more than likely be offered jobs only in nearby states, and rarely will have to travel a great distance. However, your children can be registered in other states if you desire that work.

One beautiful commercial shot on a farm in Wisconsin required a whole day to film. The children modeling on that job (and their mother) had fun meeting different people and visiting with them through their daily routines. On another farm shot, while shooting a scene on one side of a small lake, all action stopped while models, mothers and crew watched the birth of a calf on the other side of the lake. This was another beautiful experience. Such experiences make modeling memorable and extremely worthwhile.

Ad Copies

If your child makes a commercial and is not a general extra, but a principal actor, you should get a copy of the commercial on a reel of video tape purchased for that purpose. After a commercial has been aired, ask the production company if it will release the commercial to you. Then take it to a studio and have it put the commercial on your reel of video tape. Even if you don't have a video tape player, you will still have a permanent record of your children's commercials, so some day the whole family can enjoy them and they'll be able to show them to their children. For the time being, you can go to your local library and have your tapes played free at the library's video center.

A local studio might charge you $20 or more to put a commercial on your tape. If possible, you might borrow the master tape, take it to a sound studio and have the commercial copied on your tape for $10 or less! If you tell the original production company that you could get a better deal down the street, maybe they'll match the price and save you a trip. On the other hand, the original production company may insist on keeping the master tape copy, so you won't have a choice. Negotiating down from a high price may save you some money, however.

The small video tape recording expense can come out of your child's account because it's a business expense and something your child would want you to do for a record of commercials.

Personal Cameras

On jobs for TV commercials you may want to take a camera to get some pictures for your scrapbooks. Since you can usually get good copies of print work, you should only do this for TV commercials, and then only when it won't bother anyone. Try to use existing studio set up lighting so as not to disturb production crews with your camera's flash. Also, always ask permission to take your pictures. Most production people don't mind it while a shot is still being set up, but don't ever flash a camera while they're taping or filming.

15

TV Commercial Payments

You're almost always honestly paid for a commercial's use. Most clients are reputable. That's not to say, however, that there aren't incidents where a commercial is shown long after payment has ceased.

When money is scarce, a client may pay a residual and re-use an old commercial, or may even go to illustrated ads. Many times there's a big surge of modeling in December to use up a client's budget by the end of the year.

More Markets, More Pay

The amount paid for modeling in TV commercials varies. Models get a straight shooting fee which is the fee for the local market. If the client decides to use the commercial in more than a local market, models get paid a shooting fee plus a fee for each market that buys into the commercial. If the client decides to go national with the commercial, and buys into national markets all over the country, models get paid even more. Finally, if a child model is lucky enough, he or she may get a network national commercial. This means the commercial is shown on a nationwide network of TV stations simultaneously.

Residuals

Local commercials and national commercials pay in the same manner. A model gets a shooting fee that entitles the client to use the commercial for 13 weeks. After 13 weeks, if a client decides to play a *local* commercial again, the model is paid another fee equal to the shooting fee. This is called a "residual." If, after 13 weeks, a client decides to run a national commercial over again, the model is paid a residual fee equal to the original shooting fee, plus a fee for *each market* the commercial plays in. This fee for additional markets is always added, even to the original shooting fee.

Holding Fees

If a client decides to use a commercial a year from the shooting date, the model must be paid a fee for every 13 weeks that the commercial is held, regardless of whether it is aired or not. This fee is called a "holding fee." It is equivalent to the shooting fee.

A model might be in a seasonal commercial, for which there is no holding fee. The client pays only for the season—Christmas, Halloween, Easter.

National Network Pay

When a national network commercial is played, payment is entirely different. For a national network, the model is paid standard shooting and holding fees every 13 weeks, but *each and every time* the commercial is played, the model gets a fee. The model will get a payment check with a stub that indicates every single date the commercial has been played. Checks come more often than every 13 weeks.

A national network TV commercial is the best commercial a model can get. Every model dreams of this, but the competition is so great only a few ever make it. Some child models have many network nationals, but you can feel very fortunate if you get just one. When you do, enjoy your good fortune! Local, regional, and non-network nationals are a feather in your child's cap too. Keep trying and your big break can come.

Payment Timing

A client is supposed to pay a model for a TV commercial within 12 days of the shooting. When more cities are added to the original number, the commercial is upgraded and the extra fees are paid. A model could conceivably make a few good commercials and collect on them every 13 weeks for a long period of time, sometimes running to years.

Contract Life

The standard contract life of a commercial is for a two-year period. The commercial may be used anytime within this period, providing all other payments are made. After the two-year period the client must have the model sign another release.

When contemplating the big money earnings potential of national network TV, consider the long-lived *Life* cereal commercial. This national network commercial has been running for years. "Mikey," the boy eating the cereal, may possibly have made hundreds of thousands of dollars just from this one commercial. What people don't realize is that the "Mikey" model has two of his real brothers modeling with him in that same commercial, and the other two boys earned the same amount as "Mikey"! The *Life* cereal boys are all wealthy by now from that one commercial alone!

Keep in mind that in addition to the *Life* cereal TV commercial, "Mikey" and the other boys also got paid special cover rates for their photographs appearing on the cereal boxes. They've been getting TV commercial residuals for many years. The ad agency was good, and everything came together just right to cause the commercial magic to happen. "Mikey" and the other boys got paid a lot of money for an eight-hour day, and who knows, they might have wrapped it up in two hours!

Kinds of Jobs

There are as many categories for jobs as there are models. Some models can be hired to be a hand, leg, or foot model. This entails a special rate. Others can be hired as general extras where they're not recognizable. Frequently, models are hired on a "general extra buy-out" basis, which means that even though the models might be on a network commercial, they'll only be paid once. The general extra buy-out model is paid at a slightly higher rate than the general extra who is not a buy-out, but the general extra model could be renewed and paid additional fees every thirteen weeks. As a general extra buy-out, the model doesn't have any future rights.

A model can be a "principal" in a commercial. This simply means that the model is recognizable and that the model's face has to be on screen for three seconds. Also, a model may or may not speak in the commercial, but the rate is the same. In fact, the model's voice alone can be used, and there's a special fee for that.

Test Commercials

Sometimes a model can be used in a test commercial. This pays a slightly lower rate than a principal in a regular commercial, but more than a general extra or a general extra buy-out. A model could be in a test commercial that isn't supposed to be aired, but after awhile, the client might decide to upgrade the test commercial, making it a regular commercial. In this case, the client has to pay the model again at the regular commercial rate.

For some test commercials, only still pictures are shot, pasted on a storyboard, then presented to a client. The ad agency will try to sell the ad concept. However, if the client likes it and buys it, your child doesn't automatically get to do that commercial because he was in the test commercial. The client almost always has a tryout and wants to see many models.

Industrial Films

Industrial films are longer than TV commercials and involve long speaking scripts. The standard commercial is thirty seconds, but an industrial film could be five minutes or more. Consequently, industrial films pay a special rate. Film jobs generally go to more skilled actors and actresses, because there are so many lines.

There are many different modeling classifications and rates. Those mentioned are only a sampling of a few familiar ones. All the classifications and rates are frequently subject to change.

Remote Locations

Once in awhile, if a model has to go to a location that requires much traveling, the client will pay for mileage. Sometimes the crew rents a van and everyone goes to the location together.

16

Mothers:
Never Say Smile

Probably the nicest compliment a mother can receive is when a photographer or production crew reports back to the agency or tells her, "She's no stage mother!" Keeping yourself from becoming a stage mother is easier said than done!

When working for a team of commercial photographers there's one thing you learn quickly: Get a mother away from her child's view. When one of your own children models for the first time, your biggest enemy can be your own anxiety. It's easy for a mother to forget her background role and risk becoming a "stage mother." You have to make a conscious effort to keep out of the way of production crews, directors, and your child. Avoid asserting yourself or coaching your child on the set. Keep in the background and out of the way!

Stage Mother I

A mother was at a park on her daughter's second job. She was in the background but kept telling her child to "Smile!" The photographer and the art director were very polite and patient with her. She didn't realize what she was doing until the art director finally said, "He's a pretty good photographer and can usually get what he wants out of the child." Then the mother said to herself, "I've done it! I've done what I said I would *not* do. I know better and I did it anyway!" The crew went on to another spot in the park, and the mother stayed back in a little pavillion feeling very sheepish, knowing that she had just failed to avoid being "Stage Mother I." It never happened again though, and this mother learned the lesson that some mothers never learn.

Stage Mother II

At one job a typical stage mother was coaching her own son in a studio shot with about four or five other kids. All the other parents were quietly standing around watching, but when the photographer would talk to the little children in the shot, one of the mothers, at the top of her voice, would tell her son to smile, or turn, or look at the camera. It got so bad that everybody was suffering along with the photographer.

During a break, the stage mother's husband was talking to another mother, and she told him that what his wife was doing was not a good idea. She told him in a kind way that he should try to keep his wife out of the studio so she wouldn't distract anyone. When the shooting resumed, he talked to his wife, but she did the same thing again and continued interfering for the rest of the shoot. Stage Mother II's child never got another job. When she left, the other children were all reshot with another boy in her son's place. The mother of a child model has to get her child ready and then disappear.

Before a child model walks on set, the mother has an important job. But when it's camera time, the best thing a mother can do is walk out of that room. She should go any place where she will be out of her child's sight and out of the production crew's way. If she doesn't, her child will be responding to her rather than the director or photographer. This should not happen. A child must respond to the director or photographer at all times. The model is the photographer's child for a minimum of one hour, or however long the shooting takes.

Mothers must have the wisdom of Solomon, the patience of Job, and the disappearing qualities of Houdini. The child is the star, and a mother is there only because the photographer requested the child (not the mother). As a mother, you can make it easy for everyone if you just do your job and then leave. After the job, you'll come back to help change your child's clothes, sign the release form, pack your gear, and leave promptly. Don't linger and delay. Production crews have other work to do and will not appreciate your wasting any of their time with idle chit-chat.

Exceptions

The only time you should take exception to this rule is when your children are doing something that might be difficult or dangerous for them.

For example, when a child must hang by the knees for an ad, stay behind camera because you can tell by the body movements when your child is trying to let the photographer know that he or she is tired and must get upright again. The photographer might be so busy watching the whole shot, he may miss or forget your child's difficulty. Stand nearby so you can tell him. But only during the difficult or dangerous shots should you be in the studio.

When your child is a preschooler, stay somewhere in the studio if the toddler needs to see you. Usually, stand behind the photographer and let him know that you will be in back of him. That way, your child can at least see your legs and know you are there.

Moving Up and Out

Some children and adults who have been making it big locally in commercials and print work make the mistake of moving. They've earned a good reputation for themselves, but instead of enjoying what's happening to them, the first thing they do is head for New York or Los Angeles. There they become little fish in a great big ocean and most of them eventually go back home. Even some of those who have great acting credits in their background and are exceptionally good talents sometimes overestimate themselves.

It happens often with child models. Some modeling children are manipulated and their parents pull up stakes, force their children to abandon their friends, school, and lifestyle to move to the large cities where they are lucky to get occasional catalogue work while waiting for the big chance that rarely, if ever, comes. Some parents keep their children trying for the "big time" some place far from home. They not only end up destroying their children, but they destroy their families as well. The children are forced to produce like an adult. The fun they were having modeling in their home city is gone. It's now feast or famine in a strange place. The children often have to pay for their parents' apartment as well as the many other living expenses. If your children really make it in modeling in their home community, and if they earn a good reputation and are making a little money, let them enjoy it! Be happy that perhaps now your children may be able to afford the horrible expenses of higher education coming up all too soon. Try to make life a little enjoyable for your children. Set your goals a little below the stars so you and your modeling children enjoy your good fortune.

There's a whole world full of stage mothers who consider modeling to be a part of the show business life that they want for their daughters. Many of these kids do have a great deal of talent, but their talent is turned into big business, rather than remaining just fun.

Waiting Time

While mothers are waiting for their children at modeling jobs, they often visit with other child model mothers or do some quiet work. You should always have several things to do. For example, one mother started making little ribbon barrettes and selling them to local retail stores when the fad was just getting started. You might like to read, knit, crochet, mend, write letters, or do some other things that interest you.

When your children are off camera or waiting, put whatever you're doing aside and entertain them by playing cards with them, working puzzles or other quiet games. When they're doing something quietly by themselves, such as a coloring or activity book, then you can do your own kind of work. If they need you to work with them, you should without hesitation. You are there to help keep your children quiet while they're waiting for camera time, or to get them ready on time when production crews want them.

Lone Children

If other children have been in the modeling business a long time and they are quiet kids, it's easier for you to be alone with them on a job. There are mothers who are working and just can't get away long enough to stay on a job with their children. Yet putting young children on their own is really not right and not legal (see chapter on AFTRA). A modeling job is usually too long a period of time for a child to be alone. Everyone gets bored waiting on long jobs. Without something to do, you'll get restless. Nevertheless, you must be there. If a mother consistently drops her child off at a modeling job and leaves him or her all alone for the entire job, it is time that mother and child get out of modeling. It's unfair as well as illegal for mothers of models to push their own child-tending tasks on other mothers or studio personnel who have their own responsibilities to perform.

Full-time Commitment

Modeling is a full-time commitment on the part of a mother. Some mothers realize that when their children are all in school and the mother's days are her own again, she will have to get a job to help her children pay for their higher education. This is why modeling comes as a blessing. You get to do something with your children that you all like, and your children get a head start to earning their own way through college. For these reasons, you can regard modeling as your primary job, and consider it a 24-hour-a-day commitment. Your personal pursuits and volunteer, social, or charitable work are secondary. If you're scheduled to volunteer at school, and a modeling job comes up, you must postpone the volunteer work and go to the modeling job. Regardless of what other plans you've made, whether it's lunch with a friend or a school meeting, if a modeling job comes up, that should be your first priority.

Refusing Jobs

You should refuse a job if two clients want the same child at the same time. In this case, you should work with the client who called first. If you have more than one child in modeling and agencies want to book them for different jobs at the same time but different places, you will have to select one job, unless you have more than one reliable dresser, driver, and car. When such conflicts arise, perhaps you can recruit the help of your husband, an older son or daughter, or other relatives or friends.

A Profession

Regard modeling as a profession. If you do your children will also, and modeling will be rewarding for all of you. Clients, photographers, and art directors can tell when you approach modeling in a professional way, and they will appreciate it. They also appreciate your availability on short notice to substitute when another model suddenly gets ill or cannot make a job. This happens many times. Also, if you have several children and a range of sizes, you can handle almost any child job on short notice, and will be an extremely valuable asset to a modeling agency.

It is almost impossible for a woman to work full time in an eight-to-five job outside her home and still run a modeling business for her child, unless her child rarely models. Many professionals don't even go on summer vacations because that's the busy modeling season and back-to-school ads are made at this time.

As you get busier, you can compare calendars from previous years because jobs run in a similar frequency each year. Thus, if October was a busy month or July was a busy month the year before, they will probably be busy again. Unless your children have outgrown the work that they would be called to do, the scheduling will be fairly consistent. If a department store that has usually used your children during a particular month has now switched to using different models, assume your children will be less busy that month in the year upcoming. Keep in mind, however, the possibility of new jobs that could replace the old ones.

Tryout vs. Job Rejection

Rejection has been discussed in relation to commercials, but there is also another type of rejection. Your child may have a steady job with a particular department store, and has been called all year long for every shooting. Then, all of a sudden, after a year or two, or even five years, the client goes to someone else. It might even be for the same size model, so it's not as though your child has outgrown the job. It's just that the client is using someone else—a new face, a different look. This is very hard to accept gracefully. If it happens to you, you should help your children understand, but only if they seem concerned about it.

Rejection from a steady job usually occurs because the client is simply looking for a new face. Of course, you should examine your own behavior to see if you have done something wrong. Have you been a typical stage mother, or has your child done something wrong? If the answer is, "No," then you can honestly say that the client just wanted to have a new face, a different look. But knowing this doesn't make it any easier to accept. It's just a fact of modeling life. The positive way is the only way to look at it—it was a real bonanza for a few years, and there's always that next job!

Job Loss

There are many reasons why your child may lose a job. For example, one department store may use your child throughout a year, and then stop. It switches models around, using them only for a short while. There's also another type of client that uses children all the time in its ads and catalogues. After using them for a couple of years, the client moves them up to cover shots and special jobs. The models do bigger and better jobs!

It's hard when you look back in your record books and see the lovely jobs your children did for a particular store in previous years, and then realize that this year there's nothing more for that store. However, the client is boss, no questions. Modeling is a fickle business.

Bless the Clients

To summarize, you have to appreciate what clients, art directors, and photographers have done for your modeling children. What a wonderful experience your children have enjoyed! For these reasons, you should always think kindly of those you've been privileged to serve. They have given your children the opportunity to model!

Scrapbooks and Ad Copies

You should buy scrapbooks for each of your children. When they're in an ad, try to get copies of the ad for their scrapbooks. If there's more than one of your children in the ad, try to get a copy for each scrapbook, plus one for yourself. If only one of your children is in an ad try to get at least two good copies.

Scrapbooks are kept for the family, but sometimes clients ask to see what your kids have done. Usually, however, clients go strictly by agency head sheets.

One helpful ad copy aid you may want is a personal business card. When children do a print job, give the client your card and ask him to mail you a copy of the finished ad. If you don't have a business card, just give the client your name and address on a slip of paper.

17

Managing Pay and Expenses

Job Record Book

Keep accurate, careful records of all your children's modeling jobs and tryouts in a spiral booklet of index cards. You can keep your own modeling job records in this book also. (See sample format on the following page.)

Divide each card into eight columns. The left column is for job *date*. The next column *identifies the job*. Record your child's name, client name, photographer, agency (initials only) and agency person who booked the job. In the third column write in the *agency initials* again for easy recognition. Then, in the fourth column, show the *hours worked*, followed by *date paid* for the job in the fifth column, and *mileage* in the sixth column.

Always keep track of mileage to and from a job. The ideal way to do it is to note your car's odometer reading at the beginning of a trip, and then subtract from it the reading at the end of the trip. You can do that initially, but when you continue to go to the same places over and over, it's easier to put down the round trip mileage once you know it. This saves a lot of time-consuming calculations.

In the seventh column, record *gross income* received for the job. In the eighth and last column record *net amount*. The net amount is the actual amount of money you are paid after subtracting the agency's commission and other deductions from the gross amount. Write *print jobs in black or blue ink* and *commercials in red ink*. This way you can quickly read down a page and find a job record for a commercial.

Your modeling job records should be quite complete. For example, for each job, you should know who the photographer was and which agency to contact should any questions come up about payment or other matters. Also, by merely flipping through your book and scanning the "date paid" or fifth column, you can quickly find out which jobs your kids haven't been paid for. If there's a payment delinquency of more than 90 days, call the agency and check on payment.

Inside the front cover of the job record book you should list all your *agencies* and their *telephone numbers*, along with the *names* of the different people within the agencies. List *production companies*, some *mothers in the business* you like to talk with, and *recording studios*. If you have any questions, go to the book, look up a number and call it immediately.

A page in a job record book will look like the example shown on the opposite page.

Tryout Record Book

Since tryouts for modeling jobs are significant and tax deductible expenses, you should keep accurate records of them. In a different book, record each *tryout date* on the left,

Date	Job	Agency	Hours	Pd Date				Net
11/19	Tony-County Seat NF (Diane) T. Berthiaume	NF	2	1/18	25	100.00		68.00
11/25	Katie-County Seat NF (Kim) T. Berthiaume	NF	1-½	1/18	25	75.00		51.00
12/6	Katie-Prange Way Gem (Diane) Northwest Tele.	G	7	1/21	5	275.00		247.50
12/7	Molly-Voice Over, General Mills CC (Vicki)	CC	1	12/26	25	113.74		103.40
12/8	Tony-Prange Way Gem (Diane) Northwest Tele.	G	4-½	1/21	5	282.50		255.00
12/14	Katie-Anderson Windows NF (Kim) Bill Gale	NF	3-½	2/19	20	175.00		119.00
12/17	Pat-Control Data EM (Sue)	EM	1-½	7/31	27	52.50		44.62

followed by the *names of your children* who went to the tryout, *what the tryout was for*, *agency name* and name of *agency person* who telephoned you, *location* of the tryout if different than the agency, and round trip *mileage* total. (See sample format on the following page.)

As with your job record book, use *black ink for print tryouts* and *red ink to record commercial tryouts*. If your child is successful and gets the job, circle the date with ink. This colored ink coding enables you to quickly calculate the frequency of each kind of tryout for each child.

Your job tryout book might look like this:

TRYOUTS

(6/19)	(Molly) - John Anderson CC (Vickie)	20 mi.
6/22	Molly, Tony, Katie - NW Gem (Diane) A. Ichoff	5 mi.
7/7	Tony - Shakeys EM (Sunny)	20 mi.
(7/8)	Katie, (Tony) Pat - NW Gem (Diane) Golden Grahams	5 mi.
7/8	Pat - Fitting & Look - Famous Foot Gem (Diane) Wilson Griak	20 mi.
(7/10)	(Molly) - Shakeys EM (Sunny)	20 mi.
(7/22)	(Tony) (Katie) (Pat) - Prange Way Gem (Diane) Northwest	5 mi.
(7/24)	(Tony) (Molly), (Katie) CC (Vicki) John Anderson	20 mi

Year-End Summaries

At the end of your book each year, figure out the total dollars your children have *earned* in that year (gross and net amounts), then the total *paid* in that year (gross and net amounts). Also determine the number of tryouts they've each had and the number of jobs each got. Keep track of the total jobs, residuals per job, total residuals, total miles traveled for the year, and the total number of jobs obtained through each agency.

Rate Raises

You should always let an agency know when its pay rate slips below rates paid by other agencies in town. Locally, one mother noticed that children's rates paid at one agency were far below the standard rates paid at all the other agencies in town. She called the low-paying agency and notified the president about this problem. The president immediately met with her staff, discussed the problem, and by afternoon of the same day the agency was paying children the same rate as the other local agencies.

Recording Time Worked

When you get home from a job, put your total round trip mileage in your job record book. Then enter the number of hours your children worked. Agencies want to know exact times, for example, "12:00 to 12:43 P.M." The least amount of time that your child can get paid for a print job is one hour, even if the job takes only five minutes. If the job takes an hour and 15 minutes, the child gets paid for one and one-half hours. If the job takes more than one and one-half hours but less than two hours, the child still gets two hours, and so on. Recording exact times worked is important in establishing the next appropriate time bracket for payment purposes.

Releases

A release form is a document that you sign authorizing an agency or client to use the photographs, film, or tapes they've made of your child model.

You will always have to sign at least one release. You must sign a client release, and sometimes a photographer release. Good business sense dictates that client and photographer should also sign the release for it to be valid. On some forms there's a place where the client has to sign a second time for extended coverage such as billboards or cereal boxes.

Time Report/Release Forms

Most agencies want you to phone in your time as soon after a job as you can. The trend now, however, is toward another way of reporting time. One agency has its own combination release and time report form in three copies. A few at a time are sent out to models. The first copy goes to the client, the other two are mailed to the agency. When the model is paid, one copy is returned to the model with the job payment check attached. At this time more new forms are enclosed. This system is more convenient for everyone.

The combination form states the child model's name, but is signed by the mother since the model is underage. The client also signs. Job hours are recorded on the form, and both model and client will be present to catch any discrepancies. When both model and client sign the release, their signatures indicate that they're in agreement on the reported time also. This is a good procedure because there might be five models on a job, two of whom stay a little bit longer for additional shots. Without the three-part form, the agency may have to check back with you and say, "Your child worked only one hour while someone else worked two hours, why?" Then you have to explain that there were additional shots on the job in which the other two models worked, and your child didn't.

Payment Shortages

Occasionally confusion results when no forms are filled out. For example, perhaps modeling on a particular job continues 15 minutes past the hour. This means all should be paid for one and one-half hours. However, if one of the models records only an hour, giving the client the additional 15 minutes, then no one gets paid for an hour and one-half. If all the models had signed a combination release and time report on the job, the correct time would have been determined by everyone on the spot, and all would have reported the full hour and 15 minutes worked, assuring the one and one-half hour payment. Most models aren't careless about time, but to eliminate confusion and shortages, all agencies will eventually have to go to some kind of time sheet similar to the three-part combination release and time report form.

Job Sheets

Some new agencies give job sheets to models. When the model is notified about a job, the agent prepares a job sheet, recording the following information: client name, phone, extension, the ad usage, fitting, date, time, location; black and white or color photographs, single, double, triple, or group; makeup, what style; wardrobe type (season or non-seasonal), color, description, and accessories. This is a novel, unusual, yet quite sensible practice. It's a great improvement over recording all this information yourself.

Tracking Expenses

Modeling includes many expenses also. You may go to one tryout for a commercial and possibly get a callback or second tryout. Even second callbacks (or third tryouts) for a job can occur. Traveling back and forth uses gas at a time when it is no longer cheap, and your time is valuable too. You have wardrobe expenses, plus all those necessary lunches. If a child is shooting a commercial or other job that goes through the lunch hour, the client buys lunch for everybody, including parents. If you work with kids before or after lunch hour, you might like to take them out to lunch as a treat. It's also a legitimate expense since you don't have the time to make them lunch and would be too far away from home.

Managing Funds

You are the children's business manager. They each should have individual bank accounts, and money should be properly banked and invested for them.

Different families have various ways of handling their children's earnings. You might want to set up a general fund. Let your children earn up to a certain amount on each job, then the balance of money earned is put into a general fund for all the children to share, and also to help pay their expenses such as AFTRA dues, head sheets, and wardrobe. Expense of head sheets is annual. Agencies prefer that a child uses different photographs for each agency; therefore, photographs might have to be reshot for each agency.

Buy wardrobes out of the general fund. If gas and parking lots run too much in one week, you can occasionally use some money from the fund. Travel expenses may or may not be taken out of the fund unless for unusually long distances. You can deduct travel expenses on your income tax returns.

Family Partnership

If your modeling activity is significant, you may want to form a family partnership and file the 1065 tax form. This is a practical method of handling family earnings, as opposed to individual earnings. All income earned as a family is pooled and reported on a Form 1065 Partnership return. Expenses of the business are then written off, and income after expense is distributed to individual family members or partners on K-1 forms. In most family partnerships, the husband and wife are the general partners; the children are the limited partners. This method of operating can be well suited to your needs, but you should first discuss it with your accountant, and have him or her help you determine what you should do.

Rewarding Children

We all need rewards for our work, so it's very important to let your children spend a little of their money occasionally, or they will never have a chance to enjoy or appreciate what they are earning.

You don't want your children to think this is something they can be doing all the time, but every once in awhile you should allow them to buy something nice for themselves. If they're young they really don't understand what they're earning, but buying something occasionally makes earning a little more fun. Without this reward, the money they earn will get put away where they'll never see it or understand it. Keep your children's buying under control. Let them save for something special, even if they might easily buy it with one check. You should keep books on each child, and your books should be open to your children at any time they want, but to the younger ones it doesn't mean much. Given some time, however, they'll catch on.

18

American Federation of Television and Radio Artists

The American Federation of Television and Radio Artists (AFTRA) is the union your child must join to be able to work in television and radio. There is an initiation fee established by your local AFTRA. Dues above a minimum amount are based on volume of work your children did in the previous year. You may pay these dues semi-annually.

The AFTRA local in each area is run by an executive director, assistant director, and staff. Parents of children don't usually go to meetings, but adults, children and guardians are welcome. An AFTRA union local is only as good as its paid staff, officers, and members. The greater the support, the more effective the AFTRA local.

A child can work just one commercial without having to join AFTRA. You must notify your AFTRA local before your child does the first commercial. After that first commercial, your child is on "waivers." During the first 30 days after the first commercial, your child can work any number of additional commercials without joining AFTRA. However, after 30 days, a model must join AFTRA before doing the next commercial. A new member must pay the one-time initiation fee ($500.00 currently in our local) and a year's dues. The initiation fee is substantial, depending on the local, so you ought to be sure your child isn't just a general extra in that second commercial, earning only $125.00, for example. Save the money from the first commercial, bank it, and when your child gets a second commercial (after 30 days) use the money from both commercials to pay the AFTRA initiation fee. Don't spend the money your child gets for the first commercial, because without that first money, it may be very hard for you to get the AFTRA initiation fee paid.

Reporting Earnings

Once a year you must tell AFTRA how much your child model earned in radio/TV work, and AFTRA will figure your dues accordingly. You might pay one figure for earning up to $1,000, for example. After $2,000 you would pay a little more, and so on up the scale. Your payment can be divided and paid twice a year, which is helpful.

AFTRA is responsible for negotiating the rates your children are paid for commercials. AFTRA also enforces proper payments. Any disputes arising from a job should be settled through your local AFTRA office. Do not go to the national headquarters if a local matter is unsatisfactory.

Reporting Problems

If a child is only on waivers and not an official AFTRA member, the local might refuse to give any help or advice. Problems arising on a job site that need immediate attention, like stopping a commercial that has been running too many hours, could take weeks to resolve. This kind of help is useless. It's better to have your local AFTRA establish an emergency number that members can call for immediate action on violations.

AFTRA must enforce U.S. Department of Labor regulations regarding the employment of children to assure that agencies, clients, and other employers abide by the law. Children can work only eight hours maximum per day by law. AFTRA must also assure that employers abide by U.S. Department of Labor laws regarding break times, conditions, starting times, stopping times, and many other matters. Your local AFTRA is a very important authority in representing the interests of its members.

In a recent California tragedy, two children and an adult died during the making of a movie. The deaths occurred in the pre-dawn hours of the morning! Children should never have been working at that time. Yet, if the children's parents wouldn't agree to it, the client could always find other parents who would. Your local AFTRA can act to represent you in such circumstances, so that you need not risk alienating your employers when they become forgetful of work rules.

Sample AFTRA Contract

Reproduced below is an excerpt from a typical AFTRA contract relative to recorded commercials.

AA. Employment of Minors

The parties hereto, recognizing the special situation that arises when minor children are employed, have formulated the following guidelines to ensure that:

(1) The performance environment is proper for the minor.

(2) The conditions of employment are not detrimental to the health, education and morals of the minor.

It is the intent of this provision that the best interest of the minor be the primary consideration of the parent and the adults in charge of commercial production, with due regard to the age of the minor. As used in this section, the term "parent" shall be deemed to include "guardian."

For the purposes of this section, a minor is a person 14 years of age or younger.

Interviews and Tests
Calls for interviews and individual voice and photographic tests, fittings, wardrobe tests, makeup tests, production conferences, publicity and the like, for children of school age shall be after school hours, provided such calls are completed prior to 8:00 P.M. Two adults must be present at and during any such call involving a minor. Calls for actual production shall not be so limited.

Engagement
Producer shall advise parent of the minor of the terms and conditions of the employment (studio, location, estimated hours, hazardous work, special abilities required, etc.), to the extent they are known, at the time of the hiring.

Prior to the first date of the engagement, parent shall obtain, complete and submit to the Producer or his representative the appropriate documents required by state and local law related to the employment of the minor.

Parent must be present at all times while a minor is working, and shall have the right, subject to production requirements, to be within sight and sound of the minor. The presence of parent will not interfere with the production. Parent will not bring other minors not engaged by Producer to the studio or location.

Parent will accompany minor to wardrobe, makeup, hairdressing and dressing room facilities. No dressing room

118

shall be occupied simultaneously by a minor and an adult player or by minors of the opposite sex.

Producer will provide a safe and secure place for minors to rest and play.

No minor shall be required to work in a situation which places the child in clear and present danger to life or limb. If a minor believes he or she to be in such a dangerous situation after having discussed the matter with the stunt coordinator, then the minor shall not be required to perform in such situation regardless of the validity of his or her belief.

When a Producer engages a minor, Producer must designate one individual on each set to coordinate all matters relating to the welfare of the minor and shall notify the minor's parent of the name of such individual.

If a minor is at location, the minor must leave location as soon as reasonably possible following the end of his or her working day.

Guardian, as that term is used in this Section, must be at least 18 years of age and have the written permission of the minor's parent(s) to act as guardian.

Producer agrees to determine and comply with all applicable child labor laws governing the employment of the minor, and, if one is readily available, shall keep a summary of said laws in the production office.

Any provision of this Section which is inconsistent and less restrictive than any other child labor law or regulation in applicable state or other jurisdiction shall be deemed modified to comply with such laws or regulations.

The provisions of this Section shall prevail over any inconsistent and less restrictive terms contained in any other Sections of this Agreement which would otherwise be applicable to the employment of the minor, but such

terms shall be ineffective only to the extent of such incon-
sistency without invalidating the remainder of such Sections.

After reading and understanding the AFTRA laws concerning children, use them to protect your child's rights. Most
production companies and ad agencies are conscientious in
following these rules. Troubles often come from those production companies trying to do too much on too little working capital. They are not experienced enough to plan an
eight-hour day, and often they keep children working too
long in bad conditions or an unsafe environment. They often
lie about the coverage you can expect from the commercials
they shoot, and they're so inept in performing their own jobs
that your child's rights are completely ignored. *Double check*
with your modeling agency about an unknown production
company. If they have a good reputation you have nothing
to worry about. But if they're really unknown, beware.
Know your rights and call AFTRA *on the job* if these rights are
abused. *AFTRA must give you advice and assistance if you're a
member.*

Bootleg Commercials

One local experience resulted in a court case on behalf of a
child model. The boy was selected by a well-known national
client to do some "test" shots. No mention of a commercial
was ever made. Having just started in modeling, the boy
wasn't yet a member of AFTRA. He didn't have to be at that
time, since he was on waivers.

A few months later, the "test" shot became a national
commercial on television. The mother of the boy did nothing. Next year, the commercial was on again! Then the
mother got a call from the boy's aunt in New York saying

that the commercial had been running there also. The third year, the commercial was still running and finally, after three years the mother took action.

She called up her son's agency and inquired about the situation. Her agency told her that the circumstances were absolutely not acceptable and advised her to notify AFTRA. By this time her son was a dues paying union member and off waivers, but the local AFTRA wouldn't help because the boy wasn't an AFTRA member at the time the "bootleg" commercial was made!

The mother consulted a lawyer and she told him that she knew the "test" shot was being used as a national commercial, perhaps network national, and it was not legal. The boy was never paid a shooting fee or a holding fee, throughout the three years the commercial ran. The boy should have earned thousands of dollars for that commercial but unfortunately received nothing whatsoever.

The production company is now out of business because it was stealing. The mother accepted an out-of-court settlement for a minimal payment of less than $3,000. The crooked client begrudged the boy even a minimal settlement, though the boy was entitled to thousands of dollars. The original shooting fee was $50.00 for the so-called "test" shot. Lesson: Beware of phony test shots! Find out exactly what they are "tests" for! It could be your child is unknowingly doing a "bootleg" commercial.

Most clients are highly reputable, but some are not. Generally, the problems seem to come from less known, less established ad agencies that act as go-betweens. In the "bootleg" case just mentioned, a production company, client, and ad agency were all unethical. It is a most unusual case in an otherwise healthy, ethical, and rewarding industry. Rarely, if ever, would you be caught in such a situation or have to go to court. Usually, your modeling agency will do your fighting for you, since they will want to get paid too. Even in this case it's rare that such action would be required. The modeling profession is so filled with excitement, wonderful people, and rich rewards that rarely will you ever experience any problems of the kind just described. They're the exceptions, the unexpected, the unknown. But even though they rarely happen, you should beware of them.

The Unknown and Unexpected

The following job illustrates what can happen when you're called to model for a production company that's unknown to you. This job was to be a national commercial for a franchised eating spot, and it involved a young girl and two little boys.

The children were to be on location at 5:00 A.M. That should have been the first clue! All the mothers questioned the time, knowing that there is usually so much set up time and waiting involved. But the director said they'd be ready to shoot at 5:00 A.M. As it turned out, the kids could have slept another three hours and been fresh for the shooting. An extremely rude art director hushed the mothers at the start of the shoot, even though they were far away from the shooting and being very quiet. The children were in another section of the restaurant behind a heavy drape that allowed no air to enter or escape. They were enclosed in a small, stuffy area with the hot lights burning down on them. But the biggest shock of all was when the restaurant opened for business. Previously you could have heard a pin drop during the shooting. Now all pandemonium broke loose. Customers exploded into the restaurant, knives and forks clanked, dishes clattered. Yet, cameras kept rolling and the pandemonium was recorded. It was obvious to everyone, except the director, that the shooting should have stopped!

When 12 hours had passed, three mothers decided to call the modeling agency that booked the children. They went on record as testifying that the children were still on the job after 12 hours, which is a violation of U.S. Department of Labor regulations regarding child labor. The mothers were told by the agency to call their AFTRA local immediately. After 13 hours on the job, the children were finally released.

The voice quality of the finished commercial was unbelievably bad. A larger production company managed to clean it up and pull it through, but the quality was still unprofessional. The commercial never went national, if indeed it was ever supposed to, as the production company had said. Instead it ran locally and looked and sounded as if it was put together by a group of amateurs.

19

Anticipating and Avoiding Problems

Missing School

Children usually don't have any problems missing school for modeling. Teachers generally know when children are models, although you don't necessarily need to remind them when writing a note excusing the children. Usually school personnel realize what a rare learning experience your child is privileged to have in the modeling profession.

Child models are usually good students and can make up any missed school work. If you have a young one who starts having problems with school work, you can expect to have some difficulty. Keep their noses in their books and away from the TV when it is necessary. Be sure all your children make up their school work. They can take their school work to the job and do it while waiting to model, or when they get back to school or home. But they have to be sure to make it up. The worst part about modeling is missing a school party, field trip, or special movie. Fortunately, this doesn't happen often. When it does it's hard for children and they don't like it. Try to make it up to them in some other way.

Lately, clients are becoming more aware of the problems of children missing school. Some mothers have kicked up a storm because they have a problem getting their children excused. AFTRA regulations now say auditions must be after school. As a result, when there's going to be a tryout for school-age children, clients and production companies schedule it after school hours. However, when children get a commercial, they have to work an eight-hour day, missing a whole day of school. Print work is usually scheduled during the day also, because models have to accommodate the daily work schedule of photographers and art directors.

People You Meet

You'll meet a wonderful assortment of nice people in the modeling business, and parents have a good time visiting. They know that if a client is looking for a certain type, and one person's son or daughter fits the role best, that child is going to get the part. It's no reflection on the other children; it's just a matter of what the client is looking for. Most people have the right attitude, but there are exceptions.

One mother caused her daughter endless embarrassment. She would come to jobs and immediately put herself in the spotlight. At the top of her voice she would discuss her own personal life, and every job her daughter ever did. That mother and her daughter aren't around anymore because modeling is a very serious, low-key business. Clients don't like arrogant people any more than anyone else does.

Another little girl comes to tryouts with one of her parents. Both of them stand aloof in a corner, speaking to no one. This has been happening only since the girl has gotten a lot of jobs. She and her parents are missing a lot of fun because they view modeling as cut-throat competition. Luckily, they're the exception rather than the rule.

Modeling people are usually fun and open. They all need the support of each other. Without this support, your family will be the only group that will care what your children do. Talking with other modeling families and adult models helps you learn about the profession and enables you to develop and improve your children's talents.

Eliminating Jealousy

If you have more than one child, in order to minimize and eliminate jealousy, you might let the child who has the job earn up to a certain amount. Everything over this amount can be put into a general fund for the educational use of all your children. While one child is modeling for a print job or commercial, or going out to lunch with mom, the other children are at home babysitting and getting supper ready for all of you to eat when you get home. Your other children are helping you and your modeling child with the job, so they should share some of the rewards also. Having a general fund helps you share equitably with the other children.

Modeling is a partnership business. All your children have to work at it and help each other. They're each working in different ways, so a general fund makes good sense. Modeling children get to keep most of what they earn. From that shared money, many expenses must be paid, including AFTRA dues. But, your children all earn money even when just one child works. That's equitable and minimizes jealousies.

127

Avoid Recommending Strangers

Everyone wants to get into the act! You will get phone calls from people you don't even know, including people who have children as well as those who don't. People will call to ask you to recommend an agency and if they can use you as a reference. If they are people you've never met you shouldn't let them use you as a reference. Give them a name of an agency, but go no further. Agencies have enough to do on their own and don't need mothers recruiting for them.

Chauffeurs Need Training

Having more than one driver is a necessity if you have a few children in modeling. Not too long ago four children from a large family had to model at the same time. Two were modeling for an industrial film, a third was doing print work for a newspaper and the fourth was doing a commercial. The father drove to one job, the oldest son to another, and the mother drove to the third job. If the family didn't have three drivers, they would have had to give up one or two of these jobs. Consequently, additional drivers are a plus, but chauffeurs need training too.

On that particular day, the father covered the print job the youngest son was doing. While the father, a very social person, was talking to someone on the set, his little boy got himself ready for the shot. When the finished ad appeared in the Sunday paper, it was discovered that no one had combed the little boy's hair! Fortunately, the ad was for bathrobes and the little boy, hair all mussed, looked like he just got out of bed! In the future, the little boy's father is under strict orders to talk less on a modeling job and attend to the preparations of his children for their work. Chauffeurs need training!

Separation from Your Children

An important lesson is to avoid being separated from your children. Know where your children are going to be at all times.

One time, a client took some child models on location and neglected to send a taxi back for the mothers to join them. In the ad, a group of children were portrayed getting on a school bus. A young boy played the role of a studious child with glasses, and a girl posed next to him with a lunchbox in her hand. Everytime the client's back was turned, the girl would swing the lunchbox and whack the little boy on the head. When children and crew returned from the job, the little boy was bruised and very upset.

Another incident that illustrates the importance of being near your children occurred on an advertising job for sportswear. One of the little boys had to pretend to throw a punch at a girl. He was a new model who took his job quite seriously, throwing real punches at her! The client was not aware of this and didn't realize that injury was being done to the girl model. At the end of the job, when she was alone with her mother, the girl finally broke down and cried real tears of hurt and pain. Her mother should have been close to her and taken action on the first real punch!

The two incidents described above are examples of problems that occur when mothers are separated from their children on a modeling job. The mother of a child model should always be nearby, but not necessarily in the same room. It's best to be within earshot and able to look in every so often. When something goes wrong, the modeling agency should be informed. If mothers of child models are not allowed in a room, then the client and the photographer must be aware of what is going on, take proper precautions to protect all the children entrusted to their care, and be responsible for any problems that occur.

20

Modeling Checklist and AFTRA Rules Summary

Throughout this guidebook an effort has been made to describe in detail some money-making secrets that help you help your child succeed in a professional modeling career. As a further aid to help assure your child's modeling success, the following fifty reminder points are presented. These points form a useful checklist for you to refer to after you have read the book and wish to recall its contents. Also, an "AFTRA Rules Summary" has been constructed and added as a convenient review of AFTRA regulations pertaining to employment of minors.

MODELING CHECKLIST

1. A child model must be photogenic.
2. A child model must be able to act.
3. A child model must have a natural gracefulness.
4. Avoid starting a child too young if he or she lacks endurance.
5. Register with one or more modeling agencies.
6. Never pay a fee to register with an agency.

7. Get a good head shot and, if requested by the agency, have it put on the agency headsheets.

8. Modeling schools can be helpful, but they're not really necessary to get into modeling.

9. Beware of modeling school fronts for door-to-door selling.

10. Don't pressure agencies with phone calls for tryout results—if your child gets a job they'll tell you; if he or she didn't get the job, you won't hear from them.

11. If several agencies call for the same job, the rule is go with the agency that calls first.

12. If your child is in dental braces, has missing teeth, black eye, facial cuts or other temporary problems, be sure to tell the agency before accepting a job.

13. Have current and correct sizes for the agency and client; if the size is wrong, do not accept the job.

14. Accept rejections cheerfully and help your child accept them—modeling is a fickle business.

15. God bless clients—they provide you the opportunities to work.

16. Keep a wardrobe just for modeling and keep it clean, well-pressed, and fresh.

17. Don't buy wardrobe clothes too big or too small—buy the look that fits, avoid the trendy, stick with the classic.

18. Buy the clothes sales, but don't buy the "way out" or "on the way out."

19. Before a job check the wardrobe, iron it if needed, pack it carefully; check bag for adequate supplies of makeup, hair accessories, shoes, socks, other aids.

20. Be well-rested from a good night's sleep and come to a job prepared to work hard.

21. If a speaking role, models must know their lines in advance. Come to the job well-rehearsed. Speak up loudly enough to be heard, and clearly enough to be understood.

22. Strive for the understated, fresh, and natural look in makeup.

23. Develop a cheerful, happy mood—be enthusiastic and peppy!

24. Apply for a social security number and be prepared to give that number or appropriate other tax ID number to the production assistant of the commercial production crew.

25. Before a job child models must be bathed, nails trimmed, hair freshly washed and properly cut, ready for the client.

26. Get a map, good directions, and an early start. Be sure to arrive 15 minutes before "call time."

27. If you are delayed on the way to a job, telephone immediately and inform the client.

28. Never keep a client waiting.

29. Have activity things for children to do while waiting at a job—coloring book, for example. Have children *stand* after dressing to avoid wrinkling their clothing.

30. Avoid pretension, conceit, affectation—be natural, fresh, spontaneous.

31. Be professional, courteous, well-behaved at all times.

32. When waiting for camera time, mother and child must keep quietly in the background.

33. If your child is afraid of dogs or other animals, check to make sure there aren't any unleashed ones in the shooting areas.

34. Don't worry about what to do on a job. Have your child pay attention to the photographers and directors; they'll tell you what to do.

35. Mothers: never say "Smile!" Never say anything! Avoid the "stage mother" image. *Exception:* If a job is difficult or dangerous, stay close by your child; if your child is very young (a preschooler or kindergartner), always be close by.

36. Never abandon your child on a job—you may do irreparable harm to the child and you will certainly offend others, including clients, by shirking your child-tending tasks.

37. Modeling is fun—enjoy it.

38. Use a job as an opportunity to be with your child, share a lunch, develop mutual support.

39. When the job's done, sign the release form and leave quietly.

40. Request ad copies whenever you can. Leave your name and address with the client.

41. Report job time to the agency as soon after a job as you can.

42. Keep ad scrapbooks for future reference and for building a career portfolio.

43. Be prepared to wait at least one or two months to get paid for print work.

44. Keep good job records for follow-up if you don't get paid, and for income, expense, and tax use.

45. Keep careful mileage records for audition, tryout, and job travel expense; you'll need them at income tax time.

46. Keep receipts of all modeling wardrobe, makeup, and other job related expenses; they're deductible from income and help reduce your income tax.

47. Be informed about AFTRA work rules and U.S. child labor laws so that you can take appropriate action if needed to protect your child's rights.

48. Avoid recommending strangers to modeling agencies—you'll destroy your credibility.

49. Be cautious with "test" shots—find out what they're tests for.

50. A modeling career requires your full-time commitment.

AFTRA RULES SUMMARY
REGARDING EMPLOYMENT OF MINORS*

1. The performance environment must be proper for minors.

2. Employment conditions must not be harmful to the health, education, and morals of minors.

3. The best interest of minors is primary.

*14 years of age or younger.

4. All non-production calls for school-age children shall be for after school hours and completed before 8:00 p.m.

5. At least two adults must be present at and during all non-production calls involving minors.

6. Producers must inform parents about terms and conditions of employment at the time minor children are hired.

7. Prior to a job, parents must provide producer any state or local documents required by law regarding employment of minors.

8. A parent or guardian must be present at all times a minor is working.

9. A parent or guardian must not interfere with production.

10. A parent or guardian must not bring other minors to a job who are not working that job.

11. A parent or guardian must accompany minor to dressing room.

12. No dressing room can be occupied at the same time by a minor and an adult cast member, or minors of the opposite sex.

13. Producers must provide a safe and secure place for minors to rest and play.

14. Minors need not work in situations that are dangerous to life or limb.

15. Producers must appoint a coordinator for matters concerning the welfare of minors on the job, and tell parents or guardians the coordinator's name.

16. Minors must leave a location as soon as possible after the end of their working day.

17. Guardians must be 18 years of age or older and have written guardianship permission from minor's parents.

18. Producers must comply with all applicable child labor laws and keep a summary of said laws in the production office.

21

What Children Say About Modeling

It seems the best way to end a book about modeling for children is to talk with the models themselves. Below are passages that summarize conversations with four children who are actively involved in modeling. Each of the children, ages 8, 9, 12, and 14 years, describes many of the same aspects that he or she enjoys most about modeling.

Molly—Age 8

Molly likes modeling, but sometimes must be excused from school for modeling jobs. She doesn't like to miss work at school, nor does she like to miss parties and field trips. Molly says modeling is usually fun, but when she has to model in hard poses she gets very tired. One time she modeled with a teddy bear and had to hold a difficult pose. As a reward for her work, the client let her keep the teddy bear. Molly also enjoys when she models with a cake or any other of her favorite foods, because she sometimes gets to eat it afterward. After a job Molly looks forward to getting a treat with her mother. Going out to lunch is fun too. In addition to all these things, Molly likes to earn money by modeling.

Tony—Age 9

Tony enjoys modeling because he gets to see new products and pose in different ways. He enjoys going out to lunch before or after a job. When he models with food, he also likes to sample it. Tony says he likes to earn money so that he can buy something special for himself. He enjoys being with the photographers, and is pleased that he has made many friends his own age in modeling.

Katie—Age 12

Katie likes to meet new people in modeling such as the photographers and other models (sometimes famous ones). Because she enjoys seeing new fashions in clothes, Katie considers modeling as the beginning of her career as a model or stylist.

Katie is glad that she is earning her own money for her future education, and she saves practically all of it. Occasionally she has taken money out of her account to buy something special such as a bicycle, clothes, or gifts. Katie likes to see herself in print, and also enjoys lunches out with her mother. Even though she sometimes has to make up schoolwork, Katie generally doesn't mind being excused from school.

Patrick—Age 14

Patrick enjoys earning money and recognition through modeling. Seeing his picture in print gives him a feeling of satisfaction. He has mixed feelings about school and modeling, though. He doesn't mind missing classes, but his assignments from junior high school are difficult to make up. Another aspect of modeling that Patrick likes is stopping for a snack or going out to lunch.

Appendix A

Modeling Agencies and Children

The following is transcribed from a recorded interview with Andrea Hjelm, President of the Eleanor Moore Modeling Agency based in Minneapolis, Minnesota. When agreeing to the interview, Andrea graciously consented to share her extensive knowledge and experience of the modeling business as it relates to children. In addition to owning and operating a modeling agency, Andrea is a model herself with many years of professional experience. She also has two children, one of whom has done some modeling. Andrea's comments supplement those portions of the main text that described getting started in the modeling profession and working with modeling agencies.

Evaluating Modeling Potential

We look at a child objectively and seek out-going children with liveliness and sparkle in their eyes. The only way we can make our first judgment of these qualities is with a photograph that parents submit. We look at the photograph of the child to see if there's a glint in the eyes, cute little freckles on the nose, or anything else that stands out in the photo. If we see a sparkle of some kind, we'll want to interview that child. We're able to evaluate a child's potential more effectively from an interview. Our agency interviews more children than anyone else in our region because we feel it's important to meet a child and not base our judgments merely on photographs and physical characteristics.

Good Looks

So-called "good looks" are not necessarily important in modeling. A child may not be beautiful, but have a great freckled face, wonderful red or blonde hair, and be a charming model. We're looking for a face that has some sparkle, character, and individuality. A child doesn't have to be beautiful to work as a professional model. It is important for child fashion models to be slim (not skinny) because clothes usually come in slim sizes.

Evaluating Infants

When very young children come to our agency we try to determine if they are able to take direction. Some babies are directable at age two and some aren't. Toddlers are not always verbal, so it's very hard to communicate with them. Our job is to find the right model for a photographer to work with, which means we have to go by what is specified on the work order. We try to provide the best selection of models for the job.

Evaluating Older Children

An older model should know good hand placement such as a hand in a pocket or on the waist. A good model uses hands freely, and has a natural ease and relaxation in front of the camera. *A young 10–12 year old girl should stay within her bounds.* She shouldn't try to look older than she is, but act and look her age. We want people we represent to have a nice, wholesome, natural look.

The Interview

Appointments for interviews are in the afternoon after school as required by the American Federation of Television and Radio Artists (AFTRA) union regulations regarding children.

At the interview it's important the child feels secure and relaxed. What we look for is a child who is talkative, relaxed, and who can follow directions. For example we might ask the child to repeat some words that might be used in a commercial. If we think the child has that indescribable light in the eyes, that special something, we introduce the child to the other personnel in the office so that they can make an appraisal for their respective departments, such as print or television. Usually, the brighter the child, the easier it is for the child to relax and assess the situation. It is also easier for us to make our appraisal.

Photogenic

Being photogenic correlates with good bone structure. It also has to do with the light in the eyes of the child. It's that magic a child has, that liveliness, that sparkle, that soul. It comes from inside. If a child is happy and content and works well, the inner soul and exterior presentation come together.

Children can't, as a rule, have too wide a nose, eyes too close together, too long a face, or other features that are distracting. Sometimes, however, distracting features come together well and give kids great character. They may not be suited to look like a perfect child or be appropriate in a romantic shot, but they're great with a baseball cap and catcher's mitt, or posing on skates with a hockey stick.

We need a variety of kids. Being pretty or having a perfect face is not as important as having a joyful personality and a good work attitude. Those are the qualities that count. If a child has a perfect look but can't follow direction or throws a tantrum, that child is never going to work again, regardless of his appearance.

Modeling Schools

There are several points of view on modeling schools. Schools can be very constructive, and they're a vehicle for some people to get into the business because they're motivators. If people pay their hard-earned money to be in the school, they will perform. The destructive part is that not all people who enroll in modeling schools are potential models. It would be better for the students to see an agent first to tell them if they have some potential. If children have potential, a modeling school can help them. If they don't have potential then a modeling school can be helpful as a self-improvement course, though it may never make them a model. The personality, the poise of the child, the look of the child, the individuality of a child is what counts. A modeling school can't teach or give all those things to a child if he or she doesn't already have them. You can't buy them. They come with you, your family, your environment.

Head Shot

The next step which most parents have already taken, is to get a good color head shot of the child. We use children for many different kinds of jobs, just as other large agencies do in other big cities. We use children for product, fashion, and for back-to-school ads in both print and television. Some of our major clients such as General Mills or Pillsbury, like children because these clients are geared toward the children's market with cereal, snack, toy, and fast-food products. The objective of our particular agency is to find wholesome looking children whom the clients want to represent their product.

Children need only one picture to start with. It would be wonderful if they had a portfolio, but children change so quickly that most parents can't afford to begin that way. We suggest they begin with a good head shot that we can circulate to clients, because jobs aren't as readily available as they are for adults. We can circulate one picture or two pictures back and forth to clients as job possibilities arise.

Then we request that mothers update the pictures as needed. A small child's photo should be updated at least every six months, because change comes so rapidly. When a child is older, we need an updated photo at least once a year so that we can be sure that we have a good, current photo of that child available.

A child has to start with a head shot, which is a good 8" × 10" color photograph. For commercial work color is important because commercials are done in color. Much print work is done in black and white so, if parents just wanted their children to work in print, it's acceptable to have a black and white photo.

We put head photographs in a book that we publish every year because children change so rapidly. It's important that children who have successfully modeled are included in our head book because we know they're experienced and can do well. Clients rely on head books also. We don't feel it's wise for new child models to spend the extra money it costs to be in our head book, or for us to spend the money it costs to put them there until they've modeled successfully a few times and clients start selecting them.

Beginning Photos

Inexpensive department store photos are fine to start with. We don't want to discriminate against anyone because of inability to afford a studio portrait of a child. If a child is photogenic, it will show in inexpensive photos as well as in any portrait.

When a child has modeled for awhile, funds can be made available for a professional, 8" × 10" glossy, black-and-white head shot photo. This kind of photo works very well in our market.

The other option is a composite consisting of head, three-quarters, and full-length shots of the child on an 8" × 10" black-and-white glossy sheet. We recommend that parents not do a composite for children, because children change so quickly. It's an expense that isn't necessary in our market. Major markets may require composites, but we can work well with a head shot.

Full-Color Head Sheets

In some states head sheets are done in full color, but the models pay the cost. A color photo costs much more to reproduce than a black-and-white photo. Some people pay from $150.00 to $600.00 to be in a full color head book. We could never ask a child in this market to spend this much; it wouldn't be justifiable. We try to keep our book at a modest cost so more children can afford to be in it. We often send a supplementary color photo from our file to a client when it is appropriate to do so. It's far less costly for a parent this way.

We have a limitation on the number of children we can put on head sheets or books because we try to have a limited variety of different types in each age group.

Job Frequency

Timing of the first job is totally unpredictable. It depends on the child's look, the client's demands, and season of the year. Children work most in the spring, summer, and also at Christmas time. Children will get more fashion work when they wear certain sample sizes. For our agency it seems to be size 2T, then it jumps to 6 or 6X. Size 10 is a popular sample size also. For little boys the popular size is usually 12, but it can vary. I've been in the business for more than twenty-three years and find it's better to prepare children for the decline in jobs so that they don't think it's rejection by the clients. Rather, it's because their size is no longer in demand. A child should know this, especially if he or she is doing fashion modeling. However, non-fashion modeling jobs can use children of any size or age.

Catalogue Jobs

Catalogues are sometimes a little easier for a new child model to handle. The atmosphere is a bit more relaxed and the job doesn't require as much creativity. A catalogue job is a good starting point for children who are new to modeling.

Infant Work

Because babies change very rapidly, their job frequency also changes rapidly.

Most infants aren't working very often simply because, in our market we don't have a tremendous amount of infant work available. We don't do advertisements in this market for baby food products. Nor do we do ads for baby products such as diapers. In those markets that do, infants are more in demand.

Teen Jobs

The market is very limited for teens in our area. They primarily do product ads involving family situation shots, or ads for typically teen products, such as class rings or t-shirts.

Teens are between childhood and adult sizes. A teen girl, for example, who is either 5 feet 6, or 5 feet 7 inches, should be able to fit into a woman's size 4. But a client isn't going to hire a teen-age girl to replace a twenty-four-year-old woman who has poise, maturity, a great deal of presence.

The same applies to boys. Boys can't pass as men in an ad.

Older Teens

Older teens have the same kind of problem. When they grow to be adult sizes, it's more likely that they are going to work. For instance, a teen-age girl could work when she grows to an adult size. If she weighs 115 pounds, is 5 feet 7, or 5 feet 8 inches tall, and has the face of a young adult, she could start working again, but only as an adult, not as a teen. The boys, unfortunately, stay in limbo for a number of years, because men photograph so much younger than women and they don't have the advantage of makeup.

Advice to Parents

Mothers and fathers are a stabilizing force in their young-ster's life. Children normally experience rejection on a daily basis from their peers, schools, and social environment. It's very hard, however, to maintain an evenness in a child's personality when the child is involved in modeling. Many mothers are "stage" mothers who push their children in an effort to get them into stage work and modeling.

Mothers and fathers who encourage their children to listen carefully, follow direction, and perform well are very helpful. They're the nurturing people who help keep the child stable. They have to put modeling into a proper perspective as a routine part of children's lives. Modeling is a job, as well as a responsibility that children have to the client and agent. Mothers and fathers have to play a stabilizing role.

It's very important to stabilize children when they've been rejected. For example, children who have auditioned for a television commercial and seem just as good as the child who got the job, can have a rejection problem. How do you as a parent handle that? The answer is that you treat it objectively. We can't overemphasize the fact that the child is a model or a performer. Rejection is part of a model's life so it's important for parents to help put it into perspective by assuring their children that the rejection is routine and nothing personal.

Importance of Mothers in Modeling

Mothers of modeling children are very important in building success. As much as Dad wants to help, mothers are usually the ones to press the clothes, polish the shoes, get the haircuts, and keep the kids clean. Wardrobes have to be perfect when kids are going out on auditions or to a job and that's where mothers have to work extra hard. They have to make sure there are four belts and five t-shirts, plus whatever else is needed in assorted colors. They also have to keep it together and get it to the job in "camera ready" condition.

Moms are also important in maintaining stability in their children. They are actually the children's manager because we don't have professional managers for models in this market. Mothers can manage the finances of their children as well as handle wardrobe selection, make purchases of wardrobe items, and decide what's appropriate for a job. Mothers of modeling children are important in building career success.

Stage Moms

It's possible that if mothers interfere with production they could lose jobs for their children. It's best that mothers be removed from the set, yet be close at hand to comb hair, change wardrobe, or do anything else that's needed. Sometimes mothers can be distracting and a child will perform for the mother instead of for the camera. The focal point must be only on the camera. Stage mothers interfere if they're too pushy or make comments or remarks, and can be detrimental to a child's career.

Keep Perspective

One of the most important things to remember is to keep modeling in perspective. The unusual part of modeling for a child is that it's work, and most children don't work. But, child labor laws are such that they do regulate work for children. We aren't faced with problems, because we don't have enough work for children to really be detrimental to their school activities or education. Basically children have to keep in perspective that work requires their responsibility, and that they are bringing a creative and joyous aspect to what they do.

Younger children are unpredictable. They'll bring joy to the photographer along with some frustration. Older children are usually better listeners, they are very capable of following direction and they are indeed a joy to work with.

Appendix B

Photographers and Children

Your child will probably be working most of the time with a commercial photographer who shoots still pictures for print ads. Tom Berthiaume, commercial photographer and co-owner of Arndt & Berthiaume (Minneapolis, Minnesota), has consented to give some thoughts on children and modeling.

Tom is comfortable in all types of print jobs and works equally well with children and adults. He is a good source of information about modeling from the photographer's perspective. For purposes of presentation and ease of reference, his thoughts are grouped under their appropriate subject headings. They are included here as a supplementary and additional view of related portions of the main text.

Being Photogenic

Being photogenic means that a face lights up and has an expressive quality. It's the ability to perform, to communicate a thought or an expression. It's acting ability—being able to communicate an idea with your face.

Photographers Can Help

Being photogenic is a collaboration. The photographer can help. Almost all of us can communicate one or two ideas. We can look happy or unhappy, but to get all the nuances of being surprised, quizzical, or all in-between expressions, persons really need to practice on their own. You need to come in with some ability and willingness to express your inner emotions.

People can learn to be photogenic. Most people practice in front of mirrors. Being an expressive person helps, and being smart helps too.

Working with Toddlers

Most photographers find it difficult to work with toddlers. Babies are like natural forces such as the wind and the rain. They do what they want when they want. Trying to influence them is almost impossible.

Working with Children

When working with kids I try to talk to them directly and appeal to their sense of humor or natural fantasy life so that they can tap into their acting abilities. I try to get them to be a little silly, and they understand that it's just acting. If they can pretend or act with their friends, then they can act in front of the camera too. The secret is to just relax and have a good time with it.

Working with Teens

Working with teens can be difficult because it's an awkward stage in life. It's hard for boys particularly to get loose and expressive. Trying to get them to be silly or to think silly is the challenge.

I try to deal with teens as regular people and as professionals. Also I make it clear to them that they are at work and they're expected to perform. They are being paid a good fee to come do a job. They've got abilities, and they need to use them. A job doesn't depend on whether they feel like it that day, they've actually got to do it right then and there.

Good Looks vs. Attitude

Good looks are important, but not nearly as important as good attitude. I've had many good looking kids, as well as older models too, who walk in the door looking great, but they don't all have a good, professional attitude. Without a good, professional attitude looks are absolutely useless. I'd rather have an average looking person who will work hard, take things seriously and really try, then a gorgeous person with little or no professional attitude. Good looks are approximately 25 percent of the job, the other 75 percent is really attitude.

Being Slim

Slim is best for children and adults. Cameras and photographs tend to put weight on their subjects. It's better to be a little slim. It isn't as critical as when you get into action work later on in life, but being slim indicates good health to most people.

Height and Coloring

Height and coloring really doesn't matter with children. As a matter of fact, a number of the children I work with who do best at modeling are people who don't look their age, and particularly in the teenage years. Two teen-agers I work with who are 16 and 17 years old look 13. They're small, very slight for their age, with boyish faces. In the photography studio, they're excellent because they take direction so well and have so much understanding. They're actually mature, but they look young. It's beneficial in modeling to look a couple of years younger than you are, because then you're able to take direction that much better than younger models.

With respect to coloring, blondes of course will always be popular. Other coloring, however, is certainly marketable in modeling, since our industry thrives on diversity.

Hair Styles

Kids change so much and their hair styles change a lot, also. It's important for mothers to let the photographer know if there's been any big change in hair style or hair length from when we last saw their child, or from when they had their last headsheet done. It's important we know what a kid looks like this month, this week, right now! Kids may look great on a headsheet, and may be exactly what you want, but if the headsheet was done a year ago, then it's of no use now. It's important for mothers to inform agencies and photographers of any changes from their child's headsheet photo, particularly hair style changes. Also, mothers should keep in mind that standard hair styles will get their children the most work.

Most advertising is a representation of what the public is presumed to see as ideal, average, typical sort of children. Hair styles shouldn't be bizarre or out of the ordinary. Straight long hair on a girl and average length hair on the boys, parted on the side, is what's going to work best for them. Curls are fine, but crazy perms and fuzzy hair styles really won't do for most jobs.

Color Film vs. Black and White

Whether a job is in color or black and white has little bearing on child model selection. You may look at skin color a little bit in terms of the healthiness of skin, but with most kids, the skin looks great. In fact, most children look so good that they are as suitable for black and white as for color pictures.

Professionalism

To me, there's little difference between photographic modeling and stage acting. Both require an ability to project what's needed, to be very happy, sincere, and not look phony to the camera, the public. It's acting. The most valuable training a model can have is some acting or dance lessons that help a person become comfortable moving around and projecting.

Posing

There are about four or five moves, or basic body poses, that make clothes look good. Most children can learn these moves from fashion magazines or working in front of a mirror and practicing. A modeling school is not necessary. There are certain poses that look good, and that make clothes look good. Experience on the job is very helpful and we help children all we can.

Photographers tell a child how to move for a particular shot, but it's difficult to teach a child to be graceful, for example. Practice at home is needed. I can give models some ideas, but I can't really teach them to be graceful. A personal gracefulness must be practiced and learned. No one can give it to you, especially on the set at camera time. For practice they should stand in front of a full length mirror and experiment with ways clothes can be best shown. Look in the fashion magazines and see what works for other people, what looks nice. Good models frequently help one another and borrow ideas from each other. It's a good way of learning.

Makeup

Makeup is not important for little children. Usually mothers put the little bit on that's needed for young children. For teens, it would be good to know how to do eyes, some face makeup, and a bit of contour.

Selection of Models

Sometimes the client prefers to select models, but quite often photographers make the selection. For this reason, it's good for models to get to know photographers. Often the photographer or the studio will make the selection. But in the case of fashion, usually the client will make a selection based on the size of the clothing to be modeled.

Portfolios

Sometimes mothers and children drop off pictures at a photographer's studio. It can't hurt to stop by, show a portfolio, and leave a composite. Otherwise, the photographer can only work from a composite or headsheet. It helps to be able to see a portfolio. In our market, unfortunately, kids don't usually have portfolios.

Expected Behavior

I expect children to pay attention and listen to instructions. I expect them to understand what's required and try to understand the idea behind the ad. I always like it when children ask to see a layout or have an ad explained to them. They can do a better job when they understand what's going on.

As for other kinds of set behavior, of course, we don't want kids chasing each other around, goofing off, or using the telephone. Most kids are well behaved and it's very unusual to have any problems.

If children are difficult, I lose patience quickly. I have a talk with them, tell them to settle down. Kids are much more likely to be a behavior problem if their mother is with them. However, if she is away in another room and they're alone with the photographer, it's very unlikely they would cut up. We really prefer to have the mothers away from the shooting scene, because it improves the kids' attitudes 1,000 percent.

Mom's Role

Mothers need to get children to the job on time and see that they have the right wardrobe. Also, I suspect mothers can have a lot of influence with the child's attitude. Children's attitudes can be so much better when they're working directly with the photographer. Then they know they're there for work and not play. Mothers can be around the corner, in the next room, or anywhere out of sight. We usually insist on this. If there's one thing to stress it's that mothers prepare their children well. See that their wardrobe is right. Get them to the job on time, which is 15 minutes early. Get the children in their wardrobe. Fix their hair. Then, when they're all prepared, turn them over to the photographer and disappear. If they see you, they won't be paying close attention to the photographer or director.

Chicken Story

One of the toughest jobs I remember was one a seven year-old girl did for a billboard ad, clutching a live chicken. She had to hug the chicken right up close to her and get her chin right out over it. Unfortunately, chickens aren't the most lovable animals on earth. In fact, they can be downright dangerous with their sharp beaks and claws. Apparently the art director thought it would be wonderful to have a little girl hug a chicken the same way you'd hug a puppy or kitten.

The chicken was flopping its wings around and not only was it uncooperative, but it smelled awful as all barnyard animals do. The model was a real trooper. She hung in there for hours while I shot the scene.

Finally, when everything was done the clients decided they wanted a boy instead of a girl! So they used the girl's hands and stripped in a boy's head! Often, in the business, things move so quickly and so much is done with a product that much of it is beyond the photographer's control. In this case, the advertising agency people decided to make a change. However, the model was paid. For the hourly rate that the model gets, the client expects a lot of flexibility, so the model should be prepared to take the bad with the good. Modeling often has its punishments along with its rewards. Most of the time, however, modeling is rewarding.

Appendix C

TV Production and Children

Directors in television production companies have a particularly challenging responsibility. They are required to form quick but accurate judgments about how a child will perform in front of a television camera. Their judgments must be based on a very brief, three to five minute audition.

Randy Young, Director, Northwest Teleproductions, Inc. (Minneapolis, Minnesota), gives some sound advice to modeling children and their parents about the various, necessary steps in filming commercials.

The following comments were transcribed from a recorded interview with Mr. Young. They are presented here as a supplement to related portions of the main text.

Being Photogenic is Primary

Being photogenic is a quality that's difficult to define. When we look at a child and say he's photogenic, we feel clients will be pleased to have their product represented by that child.

Much depends on the ad approach to be taken. Do you want a playful looking child with red curly hair, freckles and two front teeth missing? Maybe you need a child who can walk, talk, and chew gum at the same time, maybe even dribble down the street with a basketball! Or, perhaps a minority child is needed, or a racial cross-section of children is desirable for that feeling of American strength and greatness. The ad approach is all important in evaluating a child's photogenic quality. What is photogenic for one ad may not be for another. Selection criteria for a particular ad determines much of what is "photogenic."

Minorities Make Sense

Our policy recommendation to producers is that any time we're authorized to hire three or more actors, whether adults or kids, that one or more ought to be from a racial minority, regardless of which minority. We've found our policy to be a generally good register of what people are looking for. It's not merely a matter of equity or fairness, but sound production judgment to reflect the racially diverse, American market we sell to. You can't easily sell kids tennis shoes to black parents by always showing white kids wearing them. That's not good selling sense!

Selection Criteria

When selecting models, we look for children who are quite even looking and in the mainstream, with hair not too long, a good set of facial features, an energetic smile and a brightness in the eyes. In the first few minutes of an audition, we know whether a kid's right for the part or not.

Adult actors can be coached and directed into parts. Kids have to have the ingredients up front. If they walk into the audition with their hands in their pockets or they're fumbling with their hair, they're not going to get the job. They're too introspective. A child should bubble with enthusiasm and be outgoing! On the other hand, we don't want a kid who's too aggressive and dominating.

Our selection criteria apply equally to all children. What you're selling is a kid's cuteness, and their cuteness is going to help sell the product. But if kids have to talk, ride a bike, skate board, or do any kind of tricky action, then, generally, you may have to sacrifice a bit of cuteness for a kid who can perform.

Most Important Qualities

It's most important that child models be motivated, energetic, and outgoing. Shy children rarely make it and if they do, they don't last. In front of the lights, the shy children may get scared, but we can't spend hours of expensive production time coaxing them. The talent has to produce when we say "action."

Average Children

Child models should be wholesome and average in appearance. If, for example, you need a child to play in the mud, then that's what you look for, and an average kid is superior to an exceptionally attractive child. This idea holds true for television because a child has to be believable.

Behavioral Expectations

We expect professionalism in a child, but we don't expect a lot of it. Kids are kids. We expect them to be ready to do a scene each time we're ready. We try to be patient and understanding but we feel we have a right to expect good behavior. We're fairly good judges of when they've had enough. We know when they've peaked and are not going to get any better. That's when we stop shooting.

Head Sheets

We rarely work from head sheets because kids change too fast.

We'd rather see kids in a casting situation. Since the kids who get the job are going to be seen on television, we want to see them first in an audition.

Selecting Talent

If we've worked with kids previously, and we have an out-of-town client who has not worked with these kids, then the client will usually rely on our judgment. If a client has frequently worked with the local kids, the client might pick the talent.

Sometimes it will be a committee decision between the client and us. For example, a client might ask, "Which kid do you like best for the part?"

We might respond, "We know that these three can do it."

The client might then ask, "Which one really looks the best?" Then we'll both reach a mutually satisfactory decision.

Experience Preferred

In the modeling business experience is preferred. Once, on a job we needed one little girl, but two candidates were excellent. One had no experience, the other did. We talked with the inexperienced girl for a few moments just to see how well she moved and how inhibited she was. We asked her to run up and down the conference room. "Run down and touch the wall," we said. "Then come back as fast as you can." She ran back and forth quickly, and was great. She was energetic and didn't fidget. She answered questions. She spoke up and was everything we wanted in auditioning a kid. Then came the girl with experience. We already knew what the experienced girl could do from previous jobs, and she was as good as ever in her audition.

Our choice was between the one who looked the best and probably could do it, or the experienced girl whom we *knew* could do it. The shooting would take two long days with many expensive set-ups, so the client chose the girl with experience. The client wasn't ready to gamble on a new child, regardless of how good she seemed to be. All other things being equal, in this business experience is preferred.

Stage Mothers

Auditions are hard for children. It has to be difficult for children to walk into a room with five or more adults, and have to sell themselves. However some come through our studios who have no business at an audition. We feel sorry for those kids. They walk in hesitantly and can hardly speak. We know the minute they walk in that they aren't right for the part. What happens is that their mother is pushing them into an unwanted career. We're *lucky* that there aren't many stage mothers in our market area.

When parents make the choice with their children to do a commercial, they should support their kid all the way, and do nothing but encourage. Chastising only hurts the child, and aggravates the production crew.

Directing Children

We work very well with kids, and one thing we've found is that we can't talk down to them. For example, when directing a six-year-old we'll kneel right down to the child's level, eye-to-eye, and explain the shot. Then we walk the child through it.

We don't talk cute to children. We treat them like an adult and give them the respect an actor is due on the set. Children can sense that and it makes a difference in their performance.

Actors in general need a central voice to respond to. So, kids need to know the director's name. For example, as a director, I tell kids immediately, "My name is Randy, and if you have a problem, you tell me. I'll be telling you where to go, what to do, and when to do it. If you have a question, you come to me." Kids get confused too easily if the producer says something, the writer says something, and then the cameraman says something. As their director, I've got to establish a rapport with the kids and they have to know that I'm in charge and that they need to listen to me and respect me, as I respect them.

Career Decision

The decision to perform, act, or model, should be the child's, but not the child's alone. Very few six-year-olds, for example, are going to know enough about modeling to decide to do it. If parents help make the first decision to try it, a child usually goes along with it. If the child likes it, had a good experience, wants to do it again, fine. When you get children interested, and they like what they do, they'll stay interested. On the other hand, once a child tires of modeling and says, "I don't want to do it anymore," it's time to stop. Children with a negative attitude won't do as well and won't get as many parts. Then they waste everyone's time. When children get interested in something else and modeling isn't fun anymore, only work, or if they have to do it because mom's insisting, then nobody wins and nobody's happy. It's time to stop.

Jobs for Different Ages

From ages 4 through 10, kids do a fair amount of work. From about ages 11 until 16, they won't do as much work. When kids go through puberty, they grow so fast they're sometimes awkward, and don't quite look like adults yet. It's harder for parents to keep them looking normal or average. Early adolescence is a limbo area that generally doesn't lend itself to commercials.

If an older child looks younger that's great. They're smarter. They can take direction better, they can last longer, they're stronger, more self-assured, more confident than a younger child. You can get that much more from them.

Auditions vs. Jobs

It's hard for kids to walk into a room with about 5 adults they've never seen before in their life. If children don't have self-confidence and poise they'll clam right up. If they clam

169

up in an audition what are they going to do when all the lights go on? At that time they have to do exactly what's required and make it look normal for them. For example, a child actor may have to walk in a back door, take off a sweatshirt, throw it at a mom who's in the laundry room next to the kitchen, walk past the camera, do it all in 5 seconds, and do it as if it's done every day. It's a frightening situation for a child when facing a row of hot lights, huge camera, and 20 people watching. There are technicians, lighting people, camera people, producers, agency people, client people, and a parent all in a room they're not familiar with, in an environment that doesn't even seem real. If a child can't handle an audition easily, there's little hope for the job.

If a child is good and has experience, the audition should be the easiest part. Children with experience know what a studio is like, though they don't always know what the casting room is going to be like. That's different every time. Studios are always the same. There are always the lights, always the cameras, always the preparation for some kind of predetermined action. You never know what's going to happen in an audition since it usually only involves a small piece of the job action, or perhaps a line or two from many. Sometimes auditions are for interviewing and viewing talent only, with no rehearsal of a piece of the job. Unlike jobs, auditions are difficult to predict, but usually much easier than the job.

Recognizing the Peaks

We have to be able to judge when a child has reached the point of "that's as good as it gets." We did a 60 second spot not long ago that illustrates this situation. The only principal actor was a 5 year old girl. She didn't have to talk. The ad story was a little girl up late at night sitting on a couch, watching a scary movie. She was dressed in pajamas, holding her teddy bear and her blanket. We couldn't see the front of the TV set, but we could hear voices from a movie. In 60 seconds the little girl had to be scared, but she also had to be confident, cool, and cute. She did this well and was a rarity, because as the day went on, she got better. She improved herself as she did each take and we were able to finish at about 2:00 that afternoon. She had reached a peak. We felt she had reached the limits of her acting ability, but they were outstanding limits. She did a wonderful job.

It's tough to read most children and know when they've done their best. Once children reach their peak performance, they go down fast and that's it. If you've got four or five different scenes to shoot with them, you have to make a "peak" judgment each time, because additional shooting time and expense would be a waste.

Training

It's difficult to train children when they're young. It seems they either can do modeling and acting, or they can't. When they're older and can understand the training, then they can learn to act.

Children in commercials work hard and understand what it's like to be on a job. They learn on a job while they work. There are people they have to answer to, people they have to be attentive and listen to. Modeling is hard work and the kid who does it just to miss a day of school hasn't got his heart in it. Those who can do it seem to come by it naturally. They have a rare, uninhibited quality. Other kids may be just too introverted or inhibited. Perhaps they're not expressive enough.

Much depends on how you raise a child, though a child's mannerisms and identity are inherited to a great extent. Parents must give their children self-confidence. Environment determines whether a child learns that it doesn't hurt to meet people, and it doesn't hurt to be extroverted. The child will learn when to say something and when not to say something. It's nonsense that "children should be seen and not heard." Kids are human beings, and in an audition or shooting environment they have to be treated as people and given proper respect.

Problems

There was a time we shot a spot in California and had 10 principal children staging a spring fashion show. The children ranged in age from 6 to 12 years old, and consisted of both boys and girls. In the audience were another 30 kids of all ages that were general extras. We had choreographed this fashion show, shot the commercial, and had no problem until we found out that night that everything was unacceptable because of technical problems. We had to re-shoot the commercial. We re-shot it on a Saturday and it cost us a fortune. We had to pay double time to each and every kid!

Before the first shooting, after we auditioned the kids and decided who got the parts, we handed each child the outfit to be worn in the ad. Most of the mothers said they'd take their child's outfit home and iron it.

At the end of the re-shoot I said to the crowd assembled, "Thank you very much everyone for coming back. We appreciate it, the shoot's a wrap, we're done." As everyone was leaving, the production assistant came to me and said we had a problem. One of the little girls wasn't wearing the dress from the sponsor that she was given to wear.

I called the producer over and told him one of the little girls wasn't wearing the dress we gave her. His mouth dropped and he took the chair up off the floor and shook it in anguish. The girl was wearing a dress of her own because her mother simply decided it was cuter than the client's dress. I asked the producer what we should do. We talked for a minute then I called the production assistant back over and said, "If you ever tell a soul that the girl wasn't wearing the client's dress, I will personally burn you and distribute your ashes at sea." What a nightmare! Yet, for all its anxieties, modeling is a rewarding profession.

Index

A

B

C

175